ERIC T. WIBERG

TANKER DISASTERS

IMO'S Places of Refuge and the Special Compensation Clause; *Erika, Prestige, Castor* and 65 Casualties

Island Books
Norwalk, Connecticut

Published by Island Books, USA
www.islandbooks.biz
Copyright © Eric Troels Wiberg, 2005

Also by Eric Wiberg

Round the World in the Wrong Season
(www.wrongseason.net, January, 2010)
U-Boats in the Bahamas and Bermuda Triangle
(www.uboatsbahamas.com, March, 2010)
Juvenilia – Teen Books & Travel Writing (2009)
Published Writing 1983 – 2009 (2010)

ISBN 978-0-9843998-0-2
Library of Congress Control Number: 2009913861

Cover photos: front © Bourbon Online, back © Deutsche World

Island Books, 12 Merrill Road, Norwalk, CT 06851-3906 USA

Printed in the United States of America

First Edition, Island Books, 2009

For my parents, Jane and Anders Wiberg
Nassau, Bahamas, with thanks and love.

ABSTRACT

Despite the best efforts of maritime and coastal officials, vessels carrying oil cargoes or bunkers continue to need assistance near environmentally sensitive shorelines. A recent spate of three tanker casualties in as many years brought the issue to the fore in European legislative circles. On the salvage front, this led to demands to improve salvors' compensation for pollution mitigation, as opposed to merely saving a ship. This improvement has been sought by use of the Special Compensation Protection and Indemnity Club Clause, or SCOPIC 2000.

On another level, the casualties of the tankers *Erika* in 1999, *Castor* in 2001, and *Prestige* in 2002 brought about an urgent re-appraisal of existing legislation covering what has become known as places of refuge. In the effort to improve guidelines, the International Maritime Organization (IMO), a UN-affiliate, researched, debated and, in 2003, passed a resolution to encourage coastal states to offer places of refuge. In 2004, the government of Spain, which had denied *Castor* and *Prestige* refuge, passed their own Royal Decree, defending their right to reject any vessel seeking refuge in Spain.

A composite of roughly 70 places of refuge incidents, as related to 65 vessels in 42 countries worldwide between 1975 and 2005, provides a prism through which to appraise future reactions of various coastal states to places of refuge emergencies. Given the potential multi-billion dollar cost of modern oil pollution spills, national governments, shipowners, and salvors would do well to work together to mitigate them. A standardized response to places of refuge casualties should operate to the benefit of all concerned. Whether or not such standardization exists, or can be achieved, is a focus of this paper.

TABLE OF CONTENTS

LIST OF ILLUSTRATIONS

LIST OF TABLES

DEFINITIONS

FORCE MAJEURE - Traditional concept ingrained in maritime law that a vessel in distress may approach or beach on any coast to assist saving lives and property aboard.

IMO - International Maritime Organization - since 1958 the major international organization setting standards on world shipping. Part of United Nations, based London.

INTERTANKO – International Association of Independent Tanker Owners; lobby group.

ISU - International Salvage Union; a major lobby group representing salvors worldwide.

Lloyd's Agency - Agents of Lloyd's Underwriters of London; surveys and provides market data including for LOFs, through 400 companies worldwide from London.

Lloyd's List - The daily publication of Lloyd's of London, giving details and analysis of maritime casualties, law cases, policy and legislation. The forerunner for such daily data.

LOF; Lloyd's Open Form - A one-page salvage agreement signed by the master of a vessel requesting assistance. Unless SCOPIC applies, terms usually are 'no cure no pay.'

P&I CLUB - A voluntary association of vessel owners for "Protection and Indemnity." Designed to protect the rights of shipowners against any litigants. Also a lobby group and an on-site participant, P&I representatives take up the legal, financial cause in casualties.

PLACE OF REFUGE - Defined by the IMO as "intended for use when a ship is in need of assistance, but the safety of life is not involved. Granting access to a place of refuge could involve a political decision which can only be taken on case-by-case" (IMO, 2005).

SCOPIC - Special Compensation Protection and Indemnity Clause - part of Lloyd's Open Form standardized (one-page) salvage agreement for use between Master and Salvors.

ITOPF – International Tanker Owner's Pollution Federation Limited. Responds to and advises on remedial action for tanker oil spills, for 4,500 tanker owners worldwide.

VESSEL / TANKER: Generally a motor-propelled commercial ship carrying either a cargo of persistent oil or bunkers (engine fuel) sufficient to cause environmental damage.

SUMMARY OF MAJOR SHIP INCIDENTS/SPILLS CITED:
- *Khian Sea* and *Mobro 4000*, US/worldwide, September 1986 to
November 1988.
- *Exxon Valdez*, Alaska, U.S., March 1989.
- *Braer*, Shetland Islands Scotland, January 1993.
- *Sea Empress*, Milford Haven, U.K., February 1996.
- *Erika*, English Channel/France, December 1999.
- *Castor*, off Morocco, Spain, Mediterranean, December 2000 to
February 2001.
- *Prestige*, Spain, Bay of Biscay, November 2002.

CHAPTER 1

INTRODUCTION

Prelude

On the night of December 11th, 1999, the Maltese-flagged tanker *Erika*, carrying 31,000 tons of fuel oil from Dunkirk, France, to Gibraltar, developed a leak and began to list while crossing the notorious Bay of Biscay in a winter gale. Welcomed to seek refuge in the Loire Estuary, France, the ship was limping towards shore when she broke up and sank 40 miles from her destination. At the time of the sinking, the French government's salvage tug *Abeille Flandre* was on its way to the rescue. All of *Erika*'s men were safely evacuated by helicopters from French and British Naval forces.

The ship broke in two on the 12th of December, and the bow section sank, spilling roughly 20,000 tons of heavy fuel oil. The stern section sank, while under tow from the *Abeille Flandre*, the following day. The event was widely filmed and photographed. The image of the ship's stern plunging to the bottom in a fog of haze, its propeller clearly visible, was broadcast worldwide, projecting the helpless horror of such wrecks (ITOPF, 2005, Figure 1). The oil came ashore at Christmastime along a stretch of French coastline famous for its beaches. Tourism, mariculture (mussels and oysters) and salt ponds were badly damaged. Over 50,000 birds are known to have died (CEDRE, 2005).

In December of 2000, the tanker *Castor*, carrying 29,500 tons of unleaded gasoline from Constanza, Romania, to Lagos, Nigeria, experienced an extensive hull crack off the Mediterranean coast of Morocco near Nador. Denied entry to any place of refuge, the ship lingered for a week before giving up and turning north towards Spain and a safe place to fix the problem. Surrounded by salvage tugs and tankers waiting to receive *Castor*'s cargo, the convoy was rejected by Spain. In deteriorating weather, the vessel had to be abandoned. The Spanish government assisted the crew off the stricken tanker, but denied it any place of refuge. For the next six weeks, from the day after Christmas to the day after Valentine's, *Castor* was a leper, being towed slowly east, looking for somewhere to rest and take shelter from winter gales which reached hurricane force and hammered the ship's hull. One by one, *Castor* was denied access to Morocco, Spain, Gibraltar, Algeria, Tunisia, Greece, Cyprus and Malta.

Ultimately, after the weather settled enough for the ship to transfer 23,000 tons of gasoline to another ship 100 miles from Tunisia, the *Castor* was towed to a repair yard in Greece. This glaring example of pariahhood by a tanker shocked the shipping industry. Because the shipowners did not invoke a clause called Special Compensation (SCOPIC) to reward salvors for preventing major oil spills, the *Castor*'s salvors were deprived of a third of their reward. While no coastal states stepped in to help the *Castor*, the team that did all the work and saved the ship barely covered their costs. They threatened to leave the salvage industry, which has been struggling to cope with fewer major casualties.

On the 13th of November 2002, the tanker *Prestige*, carrying 77,000 tons of heavy crude oil from St. Petersburg, Russia, and Ventspils, Latvia, approached Cape Finisterre, Spain, on its way out of the Bay of Biscay to Gibraltar and Singapore. Suddenly the ship jolted and began to heel over, listing up to 35 degrees in severe weather. The crew assembled aft, the Captain sent a Mayday, and within four hours the tug *Ria de Vigo* arrived to help keep the disabled ship off the rocks. The ship was only 26 miles from the Spanish coast, and drifted to within three miles of land. The Spanish and Portuguese government emphatically denied the owners and salvors access to a place of refuge. They ordered the vessel to steam away from land, and threatened to have the Spanish Navy and tugs tow *Prestige* away. The Portuguese Navy was placed on high alert. The crew were evacuated, and tugs attached. The Captain was arrested.

During the following days, tugs dragged the *Prestige* farther out into the Bay of Biscay and the North Atlantic, lashed by vicious winter gales for which the region is known. Seven days after the initial mishap, the *Prestige* broke in two. Within hours, both sections of the hull succumbed to the massive seas and sank 140 miles west of Vigo, Spain, taking with her some 55,000 tons of crude oil. The balance of her cargo had escaped into the sea during the salvage. Eventually it spread along a huge, 1,900-kilometer swathe of coastline in Spain, Portugal and France. For the next two years, the hull continued to emit up to 40 tons a day of sludgy fuel from three miles below the surface. Two years later, the last 15,000 tons of her cargo was siphoned out of the hull at 12,000-foot depths using groundbreaking technology. The cost of cleanup is estimated to be five billion Euro dollars, or roughly $6.5 billion U.S. dollars in April 2005.

Understandably, these incidents have sparked passionate debate. Since existing law already covered most aspects of the mishaps, investigators and the public looked for weak spots in legislation. There seems to be consensus that one weak spot deals with places of refuge. The UN-affiliated International Maritime Organization (IMO) drafted a solution. Counter-proposals were put forth by the government of Spain. The two groups are at loggerheads. Whose solution prevails may depend on when, and where, the next major oil tanker spill occurs.

The IMO Places of Refuge Resolution of 2003 does not have any affirmative duties and is, strictly speaking, unenforceable; something termed 'aspirational law;' an act that should be done volitionally, but is not mandated. The Spanish fine-based Royal Decree of 2004 may be deemed to contravene precepts of international law dealing with freedom of the seas and *force majeure*, concepts enshrined in maritime law since the days of Hugo Grotius. This paper proposes to trace the development of salvage law through the prism of rewarding salvors, with a view to permitting them to drag their leaking quarry into welcoming places of refuge, which some countries, among them Norway and the U.K., have already designated.

Both *Erika* and *Prestige* were heavily photographed, engendering broad familiarity with, and focusing attention on, the wrecks. This persists today. To use a term from popular science,

13

Erika, *Castor* and *Prestige* are the charismatic *mega fauna* of 21st century shipping, meaning they are the media persona that draws public attention to a cause or crisis (typical *mega fauna* are whales, bears, and eagles, each bringing attention to wider environmental issues). This triumvirate of wrecks is Europe's equivalent of the *Exxon Valdez,* which led to legislation in the form of OPA 1990. These casualties focused Europe's legislative attention on the issue of shipping reform to a degree that had not been seen since the huge *Amoco Cadiz* and *Torrey Canyon* spills of the 1960s and 1970s. There are laws on the European Union's books named after *Erika.*

Within the salvage industry, there has been a sea change in recent decades. Driven foremost by a desire for profit, and interested in policy only inasmuch as they do not wish to be overregulated, the industry, represented by the International Salvage Union, or ISU, found itself without enough oil tankers to rescue, and with not enough reward for those that it did rescue. This fundamental tension, illustrated by several classic cases (such as *Castor*) laid the foundation for the Special Compensation Protection and Indemnity Clause (SCOPIC), which is in active use today. The challenge has been for the ISU to convince its customers of the need to offer higher incentives, and to risk making higher payouts, in order to protect the environment from oil spills.

The salvage and shipping industries need to convince the general public that a financial security net between they and the coastline may be the only skein keeping the oil off their coasts. To this end, the ISU has been actively lobbying and promulgating statistics and accomplishments on their web site and at various shipping conferences. They are, by their own accounts, being starved of work by the paucity of major oil casualties – the result, ironically, of much more stringent tanker regulations. By contrast, the 1970s were a kind of heyday for oil spills. The *Amoco Cadiz* wreck off Europe in 1978 spilled 227,000 tons in the English Channel. In July, 1979, the Very Large Crude Carriers (VLCC) *Atlantic Empress* and *Aegean Captain* collided north of Tobago, spilling over 287,000 tons of burning crude oil into the ocean north and east of Barbados.

There are statistically fewer tanker casualties in the 21st century, yet legislative, environmental, and public scrutiny has never been so intense. Although ships transport more than ninety percent of the worlds' goods, and tanker spills account for as little as three percent of oil pollution in the oceans (runoff is the biggest culprit; ITOPF, 2005 and Intertanko, 2005), oil tanker spills have a unique way of galvanizing public opinion against shipping. Despite efforts to draft what are jokingly called 'no sink' laws, most lawmakers agree that the protocol on whether to grant refuge to an at-risk ship is a delicate one, to say the least. Pragmatism and good communication seem to be the best tools for moving forward with the Places of Refuge Resolution, which presently seems locked in a standstill with Spain's Royal Decree inasmuch as the two directly conflict.

Once legislators realize that they can ban tanker accidents any more than one can ban car accidents, rules need to be made to assist vessels that are in distress and pose a risk to the environment. One such option is to establish a system whereby ships can be assured that certain ports, or places of refuge, will be designated for them to effectuate repairs. Another is to work closely with coastal states and encourage them to publish lists of places of refuge, and then to have the political fortitude to open them to ships in distress. This paper is an analysis not just of SCOPIC and IMO, but of how some seventy ship casualties over the last 30 years have been treated by the governments of more than 42 nations, or coastal states.

So that the reader may absorb the visual impact of photos to which a large portion of the world's readership and viewership were exposed during Christmas 1999, Figure 1 on the following page depicts the tanker *Erika*, broken in half, in its final throes before plunging to the depths and disgorging most of its cargo along the French coast.

Statement of the Problem

Three tanker ship casualties; *Erika*, *Castor* and *Prestige*, occurred in European waters in the space of just over three years, in 1999, 2000, and 2002 respectively. They seem to have taken European and international regulators by surprise, all the more so because of the efforts of governments and salvors to anticipate and mitigate the environmental damage. These maritime casualties focused attention on sensitive issues of national sovereignty, contrasting this to the perceived duty to help protect neighbors' coasts. Regulators found themselves euphemistically caught in the middle of an often political and less often practical, tug of war between ships, their salvors, and coastal states trying to protect their shores from unwanted oil spills with disastrous environmental and economic potential.

In trying to regulate a protective boom around their coastlines and citizens, national governments such as Spain found themselves up against angry lobbies of merchant tanker owners and an international consortium of salvors and insurers. Public outrage at the tanker spills has been so strident, and the calls for the reform of various laws – from oil spill response plans to efforts to reward salvors and to create pockets of refuge for distressed ships along the coast – that a hardening of positions has developed between two camps. On the one hand are the International Maritime Organization (IMO) and the various, mostly commercial, constituents it represents, and on the other are national governments such as Spain and France, who desire to protect their coasts at whatever cost, even if doing so is contrary to customary notions of maritime law.

Into this amalgam, legislators insert themselves, struggling to gain consensus and to batten down the hatches sufficiently and in time to survive the next onslaught. The next media maelstrom about shipwrecked, stranded, or abandoned vessels and the pollutants they carry can be unleashed without warning. As requirements for vessel safety and double-hulls come on stream into the start of the 21st century, laws and regulations are become

FIGURE 1:
PHOTOGRAPHS OF MT. *ERIKA* SINKING, 1999
Sources: <u>Lloyd's List</u>, (2005bb), CEDRE (2005), Besco (2005),
Corrosion Doctors.org (2005)

increasingly crucial. The ability to enforce them, or extract penalties for malfeasance across international borders, is equally important. As the war of wills escalates, the cost of such mishaps is also rising – the *Prestige* spill of 2002 to 2004 is projected to cost over US$6 billion. Spain now requires bonds of up to US$500 million for the privilege of approaching their coast in a distressed or disabled vessel.

Whatever regulatory lull was enjoyed following the *Exxon Valdez*, for Europe at least, has evaporated, as the nations abutting the Bay of Biscay, Mediterranean Sea, North Sea and the Baltic Sea continue to grapple with repeated threats of oil spills and their expensive consequences. This paper seeks to analyze what is being done in response to these recent oil spills, and whether it is enough. In the instance of the IMO's Places of Refuge Resolution, an interesting question remains open; to test and see if this new legislative tiger has teeth when pitted against the domestic laws of coastal states.

Sub-Problems

1) To protect the environment, is it necessary to assure salvors of their reward, not just for saving the ship, but for limiting oil pollution? Rewarding salvors both rewards the environment and also spares governments the expense of direct mitigation. Protection and Indemnity clubs (P&I clubs, or insurers, who cover shipowners) are crucial participants in the Special Compensation Protection and Indemnity Clause, or SCOPIC. P&I Clubs often represent the owners in litigation and policy formation, and end up footing the bill on behalf of a pool of contributing owners that they represent for any failure to contract sufficiently, i.e. by Lloyd's Open Form salvage agreement, to protect shipowners or salvors.

2) What are the weaknesses of Articles 13 and 14 of the 1989 International Convention on Salvage (Salvage Convention)? Is SCOPIC the sensible and practical resolution of the accounting difficulties created by adherence to the Articles? SCOPIC 2000

will be compared closely with Articles 13 and 14 of the Convention, using case studies of the contrasts between two recent tanker casualties; *Castor* (without SCOPIC) and *Prestige* (with SCOPIC).

3) The IMO's 2003 Places of Refuge Resolution: Is it sufficient to protect coastal states from repeating a blunder such as Spain's during the *Prestige*, or is it a toothless tiger? An analysis of the impact of the *Erika, Castor* and *Prestige* incidents on formulation of this new resolution, with a view to determining whether the IMO resolution would prevent another *Prestige*. Review of roughly 70 places of refuge case studies during the last 30 years will provide basis for analysis.

4) Should coastal states be asked, or required, to permit ships a place of refuge? In the absence of clear, enforceable laws, should the decision be relegated largely to the arena of political jousting in response to public debate? The data available are fourfold: 1) records of actual legislation passed (i.e. by IMO, Spain and the European Commission [EC]); 2) records of ships denied or granted places of refuge since 1975, 3) records of successful ISU salvages in which salvors have received special compensation since 1999, and 4) records of the public debate.

5) Should published lists of country's places of refuge, which are only in their fledgling state, be encouraged, despite potential retribution and local protest? This is a natural sub-category to determine not only what has occurred, but to predict, based on performance to date, what may happen in the future. Which countries are on board IMO's resolution, and which plan to be? This can be a reliable indicator of how mishaps like the *Prestige* are likely to pan out as such casualties inevitably re-occur into the future.

6) Does any of this legislative activity, whether by the IMO, European Commission or Spain, really matter? Is there in fact a precedent which has overtaken *force majeure*, developed through time-honored customary practice of the sea, whereby coastal states retain the exclusive right to determine which ships to grant, and which to deny, access to places of refuge strictly on a

case-by-case basis? If so, does this not seriously undermine the IMO's Places of Refuge Resolution? This is the ultimate question of the study.

Hypothesis

It is hypothesized that the IMO Places of Refuge Resolution, passed in late 2003, if enforced and adhered to, would have mitigated and perhaps prevented the spillage of oil from the tankers *Castor* and *Prestige*. Earlier, more decisive action by various governments at the time would have resulted in less oil spillage and the resultant environmental damage by providing places of refuge and preventing the *Prestige* from sinking at all.

The decision to force the tanker *Prestige* from the Spanish coast contravened traditional concepts of *force majeure*, a customary law embodied in admiralty law. Doing so ultimately led to greater environmental damage than if the ship had been granted a sheltered haven to offload and transship cargo. Forcing the ship to sea resulted in a scatter effect of oil which environmentally harmed a far larger swathe of coastline than if the ship had been promptly contained along the coast. As the ship was towed farther from the coast, the vector or coastline that the oil affected grew proportionately. Prompt containment of the vessel along a specific coastal bay or harbor could - and probably would - have contained the spill to the extent that it would not be the ongoing environmental disaster that it has since proved to be.

Based on spill results from 26 ships that were denied places of refuge since 1977, however, including the *Castor* mishap the year before, Spain may have been justified in taking such a risk. Based on the actual results, though, all parties would agree that Spain lost their gamble in ordering the *Prestige* away. The costs have been staggering; billions of Euros, and long lasting; over two years.

A three-stage analysis is provided. Firstly, whether SCOPIC helps the environment by helping salvors. This is the difference between Articles 13 and 14 and SCOPIC, as well as the difference in results between the *Castor* and *Prestige* incidents. Secondly, whether new legislation is required. Since the inception of this paper in 2003, such legislation now exists: IMO's Places of Refuge (2003), and Spain's Royal Decree (2004), which supervened the European Commission (EC's) *Erika* Packages. Thirdly, an assessment regarding which of these two acts has the stronger force of law is necessary.

Given that SCOPIC is now widely available to salvors, and the IMO has moved international law closer to offering places of refuge, some coastal states have hardened their defenses with punitive legislation. The question remains – what will be the result? Based on these previously stated premises, the overriding question is: Where do salvors, the environment, and coastal states stand in 2005? To answer this, roughly 70 incidents of ships being denied or granted places of refuge, and the consequences, will be studied.

Sub-Hypotheses

The question of how to cope with major shipwrecks along coastal states has been brought to the forefront recently by several much-publicized nautical casualties. Two recent environmental calamities (*Erika* and *Prestige*) and a third, highly embarrassing near-miss (*Castor*) have galvanized attention on the issue of places of refuge. The sheer scale and expense, and the international nature, of major oil spills make coping with such disasters – and ideally preventing them – a top priority. The consequences of such a spill can drain national coffers, topple popularly elected governments, and cause major re-writes of both domestic and international maritime policy. Whereas in the past, the focus was on saving the crews and salvaging the ships, nowadays the greatest priority is shifting to preventing oil cargoes and bunkers from leaving disabled ships' hulls and smearing hundreds of miles of coastline.

As the *Prestige* disaster proves, a few days of poor decision-making on a national level, inadequate international law, and poor intergovernmental communication can have major deleterious effects on the environment and governments for years afterwards. These effects are most glaringly felt on environmental, political, and economic levels. Ultimately, it pays to protect the shoreline with well-thought-out, effective legislation, a salvage infrastructure which is willing and able to act to prevent spills and can reasonably expect to be paid for their services, and pre-agreed cooperation on an international level.

After three major mishaps in three years, it is evident to European coastal states that tanker accidents are regrettably very real, even imminent prospects. Providing places of refuge, where shelter can be sought and remedial measures taken, has taken on a new appeal. Getting governments to agree on which corners of their coasts would be sacrificed to provide places of refuge is less easy. To test this overall hypothesis, it is helpful to break it down into six sub-hypotheses dealing with specific aspects of the overall theme. This way, each component can be tested, evaluated, and concluded upon. A synthesis of all six tests rounds off this study, provides insight and suggestion, and arrives at conclusions which may well seem surprising, provided their original premises.

H-1) In order to protect the environment, it is helpful to ensure that the salvors doing the physical protecting of coastlines are properly awarded. SCOPIC sets out to improve on Articles 13 and 14. Whether it achieves this is studied in detail.

H-2) The *Castor* episode exposed the weaknesses of Articles 13 and 14 of the Salvage Convention, particularly in the final reward, which was arbitrarily cut by one third. Articles 13 and 14 and SCOPIC is critically studied, compared and contrasted. They are tested against actual cases to see if SCOPIC really is the best way to protect salvors, and, concomitantly, the environment.

H-3) The IMO Places of Refuge Resolution has the potential to prevent a present-day repeat of the *Prestige*. Will it? Does it have the force of law? Or will common practice, as evidenced by some 70 case studies, prevail, leaving the coastal state with the ultimate decision on whether to accept or reject vessels in distress?

H-4) Taken in conjunction, the *Erika, Castor* and *Prestige* incidents focused attention to the issue of places of refuge and governmental responsibility for oil spills in a way that had not been experienced on such as scale since earlier wrecks such as *Torrey Canyon* (1967), *Amoco Cadiz* (1978), *Exxon Valdez* (1989), *Sea Empress* (1996), *Braer* (1993), and others. A careful study of legislative intent, media inputs, and governmental and non-government-organization-commissioned studies (CMI, 2002, and IMO, 2005) supports the need to identify and list places of refuge. Several countries have already tentatively promulgated such lists. A series of attempts to improve the European Commission's position were in fact named the *Erika* packages after one of the casualties.

H-5) A determination of which countries have voluntarily allocated places of refuge, or have promised to do so, serves as an indicator of whether the IMO resolution will be effective. Using 66 case studies over the past 30 years, it is possible to deduce certain track records for nations' performance as regards offering or denying places of refuge.

H-6) The IMO Places of Refuge Resolution, the European Commission's three *Erika* Packages, and Spain's punitive 2004 Royal Decree, will have a real effect in altering the behavior of coastal states in the face of distressed ships. This is the intended result of the new directives. Recent case studies should provide sufficient indicators of whether the new legislation is having a positive effect.

Background and Significance of Study

This study will be significant because it recognizes and analyzes an important new area of legislation; that to protect the environment, governments need to assure salvors that their labor will be rewarded. In order to assist salvors, salvage masters aboard stricken vessels should be provided the option of seeking a place of refuge. It is important to realize that for centuries, and particularly since the advent of steam ships and oil tanker ships in the 20th century, virtually every other aspect of modern ship operations have been regulated. These include ship design, construction, maintenance and classification, including engineering, manning, crewing, supply, bunkering (re-fuelling), bridge navigation, watch-standing procedures, safety of crew, ship and cargo, and electronics. Likewise, the rescue of personnel is carefully regulated, with specific allocations of search and rescue (SAR) resources worldwide on inter-dependent regional and local levels.

An interesting question arising from this research is what to do *after* the safety of life at sea convention (SOLAS) is negated by removal of the crew. In other words, what to do with an abandoned, derelict vessel operating literally not under command (a term from the Collision Regulations, or COLREGS), which is a serious, immediate threat to not just the oceanic, but the coastal environments, as well as a hazard to shipping. Because the time window for such casualties is often very narrow, urgent, decisive action is often required to avoid or mitigate environmental calamity. The thorny issue of coastal state rights versus the rights of salvors must have clear mandates from international and national governmental organizations.

Some nations, such as France, the U.S. and Singapore, have very clear procedures and SAR capabilities, which include coast guard resources, fixed wing and helicopter aircraft, naval resources, and ocean-going tugs with heavy tow and boom-deployment capability. Other nations are not as well equipped for such a response. Though some recent data exists, places of refuge proposals have not been exhaustively tested since the *Prestige* and *Castor* mishaps. With a major focus on mitigation of environmental damage, resulting from the release of persistent oil pollutants, public attention and policy has shifted from simply life-saving and ship-saving to coast-saving measures. 'Keeping the oil in the ship,' is a mantra of the largest salvage union.

Damage from cargo spillage vastly exceeds the value of any one ship or cargo. Whereas historically it might have been enough to legislate to prevent mishaps, and focus on life-saving and ship-salvage, this is no longer the case. The cargo must be contained. Governments must work to enforce laws that will ensure the cargo will be contained, even if a comparatively small area of coast must be damaged to prevent a larger swathe from suffering pollution. This can be a difficult concept for governments, particularly their coastal-dwelling citizens and fishermen, to accept. The balancing of harms is of crucial importance not only environmentally, but politically.

The notion that oil spills from ships can be legislated out of existence is nefarious. It is also continuously and repeatedly proven to be unrealistic. Even with double hulls, the nature of maritime trade, and the necessity that they be manned by humans, with their inherent flaws, ensures that the world will continue to experience ship-borne oil spills. The international legal body's task is tantamount to damage control. Like a surgeon-general, they are moving from one aspect of shipping; double-hulling, search-and-rescue, classification, and flagging regulations, to another; dealing with the results of any failures in earlier efforts. Once the first barrier of laws has failed, and a ship is actually disabled in proximity to a coast, procedures must exist or response patterns must be in place to enable coastal states to deal with minimalizing pollution damage through concerted communication and action.

As the traditional remedy of *force majeure* is rendered moot by the removal of the crew, new policies must be written to deal with the consequences of errant, unmanned ships, their cargos and bunkers. The Places of Refuge Resolution represents an earnest effort by IMO in that direction. Whether it will work will be analyzed against casualties that have already occurred (*Castor* and *Prestige*). An effort to extrapolate and project its future viability is made. However, the world will not know whether this places of refuge resolution is effective or not until the next, inevitable oil spill casualty.

This study is particularly relevant in light of the fact that world economies - particularly those of the U.S., Europe, and the growing economies of China, Southeast Asia, and Africa steadily increase their demand for liquid petroleum in crude and product (refined) form. Whatever alternative energy proposals have existed since the awakening of environmental consciousness in the 1960s and 1970s, there do not appear to be viable alternatives in 2005 for the transport of massive volumes of liquid petroleum by the worlds' tanker fleet of over 10,000 tankers and 350 million deadweight; DWT or cargo-carrying capacity in tons (ISL, 2005).

The recent high cost of oil products like gasoline and diesel in the U.S. and worldwide is an indication of this continued demand. The congressional vote to open the North Slope oil fields, in the Arctic preserves of Alaska, to drilling in 2005, after decades of contentious debate, further illustrates this reality. The world depends on oil, and it depends, to the extent of 90 percent, on transporting it by ship. It must also protect itself from the consequences of catastrophic mishaps in the course of such transportation. The Places of Refuge Resolution is a creative, and possibly effective, way to anticipate and contain the reality of continued tanker ship transport along coastal states.

Figure 2, on following page, provides a visual of how many tons of pollutants that members of the International Salvage Union claim to have recovered between 1994 and 2004. The graphic enables the reader to compare the *Exxon Valdez, Sea Empress* and *Braer* spills with the 734,582 tons of pollutants recovered in 266 salvage operations during 2004 alone. Overall, the ISU claims to have recovered almost 12 million tons of pollutants in ten years, a remarkable feat if true. Crude oil recovery accounts for half a million tons, or 60 percent. One can only presume that the salvage of the *VLCC Orpheus Asia*, laden with 240,000 tons of crude when towed to an anchorage in Indonesia in 2002, was not accounted for in the pollution prevention analysis (Oil Spill Intelligence Report, 2002).

**ISU: RECOVERY OF POLLUTANTS
BY MARINE SALVORS – 2004**

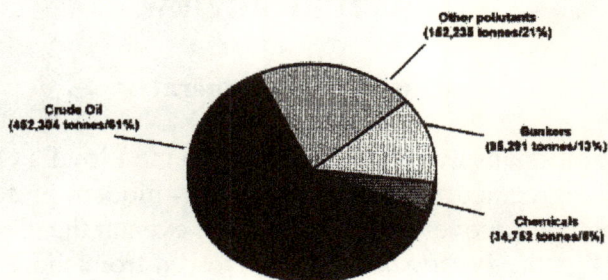

Other pollutants
(152,235 tonnes/21%)

Crude Oil
(452,304 tonnes/61%)

Bunkers
(95,291 tonnes/13%)

Chemicals
(34,752 tonnes/5%)

Exxon Valdez spill: 37,000 tonnes

Sea Empress spill: 70,000 tonnes

Braer spill: 85,000 tonnes

265 salvage operations
Pollutants recovered: 734,582 tonnes

ISU **Annual Pollution Prevention Survey**
INTERNATIONAL
SALVAGE UNION
11,742,506 tonnes of oil, chemicals and other pollutants
recovered in the 1994-2004 period

**FIGURE 2
ISU RECOVERY OF POLLUTANTS BY MARINE
SALVORS 2007**
Source: ISU, (2005f)

27

CHAPTER 2

LITERATURE REVIEW

Salvage Law in General

The traditional salvage model based on the Lloyd's Open Form (LOF) agreement is being enhanced by modern preferences for pollution control over property salvage, even at the expense of the vessels like the *Prestige,* which was towed from shore and sank in 2002. Though salvage itself is as ancient as maritime commerce, this paper deals with developments in the salvage industry since the mid-1970s; a time of increased environmental awareness, and particularly since 2000. One question is whether the salvage industry, represented in large part by the International Salvage Union (ISU), is prepared to adopt to - and governments are willing to fund and support - this shift.

In a paper by their president, the ISU warns of 'The dangers of complacency:'

During the 1970s there were over 20 significant oil spills every year. In 2002 there were just three. The improvement in the tanker industry safety and environmental record can only be described as remarkable. Is more regulation really the answer at this point? The new focus should be on prevention. Effective salvage intervention is one possible solution addressing natural perils and human error. Whether or not these perils can be eradicated by rule-making remains in question. There is, of course, no room for complacency. Salvage operations in 2002 included the first laden VLCC for four years. The number of tanker salvage cases in 2002 more than doubled, up from 19 to 39. The number of ship-to-ship transfers rose from 15 to 35 [often in Places of Refuge] (ISU, 2005, 3).

To understand this conflict and how it has played out in changing drafts of the Lloyds Open Form, it will be informative to follow the ten drafts in the past ten decades, as well as to conduct analyses of select clauses.

After the Romans, ocean travel remained notoriously dangerous, but by the early 1600s it had become common enough that the Dutch East India Company felt compelled to hire a local lawyer named Hugo Grotius (1583-1645) to write *Mare Liberum*, a carefully reasoned defense of international freedom on the high seas, based on concepts of 'natural law.' This defense of an act of piracy turned out to be the starting point of modern international maritime law. In the 1990s, officials continued to see the ocean in tidy governmental terms as a place subject to civilization, where navies projected national power and merchant ships sailed, however reluctantly, under increasing technical restraints (Langewiesche, 2004, 34-37).

The Maritime Law Association of the U.S. observes that "the increased reliance on P&I Club input during salvage operations, and the increasing role of the P&I Clubs in salvage situations is a result of fundamental changes in the nature of salvage, resulting from environmental concerns" (MLA, 2000). Defending the industry before the United States Supreme Court last year, Rhode Island legal scholar Jonathan Gutoff and his colleague Stephen White contributed that

Of particular importance to the public is the considerable amount of environmental harm the salvage industry has helped to prevent or minimize worldwide. ...This dwarfs the 37,000 tons of crude oil that was spilled when the *Exxon Valdez* grounded in Alaska in 1989, or the 77,000 tons lost when the *Prestige* sank off the coast of Spain. A party performing salvage is entitled to an award,

29

enforceable either *in rem* or *in personam* up to the value of the salved property. Compensation as salvage is not viewed by the admiralty courts merely as pay on the principle of *quantum meruit* or as a remuneration *pro opere et labore*, but as a reward given for perilous services, voluntarily rendered, and as an inducement to seamen and others to embark on such undertakings to save life and property (White, Gutoff, 2004, 1-2).

Of course one market participant unlikely to lack an opinion is the ISU:

Since 1994, when the ISU annual Pollution Prevention Survey began, our members have recovered around 12 million tons of pollutants from marine casualties. It is incumbent on salvors, port authorities and all other parties involved in casualty response to cooperate more fully, with the aim of preventing the next *Prestige*...

Regarding increasing SCOPIC rewards for pollution prevention, the ISU notes:

The (recent) failure to increase the (pollution prevention reward) rates was discouraging – contrary to the intention of SCOPIC. ISU called on Salvage Arbitrators to place greater value on the salvors' work to prevent pollution. "Pollution prevention is only one of ten criteria used by Arbitrators to arrive at Salvage Awards. It receives no special attention in this process. We believe it is now time to place a much higher value on pollution prevention, to reflect the concerns and priorities of governments and the public at large. We ask for the insurance communities' support, as they have a major interest in continued strong performance by salvors in the area of spill prevention" (ISU, 2005, 4).

The Special Compensation P&I Club Clause (SCOPIC) seeks to remedy some confusion generated by the International Salvage Convention of 1989, particularly Articles 13 and 14. SCOPIC seems to have created a degree of harmony and communication among shipowners and their P&I Club representatives. However, as will be illustrated by the cases of the *Castor* and *Prestige*, both parties have received little or no cooperation from the governments to whom oil pollution casualties are an imminent threat, particularly during the period of greatest danger. As evidenced, political forces and media pressure may complicate even the best salvage compensation awards systems, such as the Salvage Convention and SCOPIC.

The salvage industry is an integral and essential participant in maritime transport, as supported by evidence of thousands of recent successful salvages that saved tens of billions of dollars and prevented thousands of tons of pollutants from entering the sea. Two salvage vessels alone saved over 300 ships in 20 years. Between 1979 and 1998, the *Abeille Flandre* alone went to 703 rescues from Brest, France, effectuating 176 salvages. Her sistership the *Abeille Languedoc*, from Cherbourg France, set out 568 times and saved 130 vessels. Both of them prevented tremendous potential damage to environment and commerce in the English Channel (Hamon, 2003). In fact, the *Abeille Flandre* was racing to the aid of the *Erika* off the Loire estuary when she sank in 1999.

As a result of uncertainty over whether salvors will actually be paid their just rewards under various contracts, the highly capital-intensive industry has been forced to take on a serious self-evaluation since 2000. "Salvage has become a complex balance of maintaining adequate equipment and expertise, together with strong partnerships and good legal and financial backing. Salvage as a core business for any company is not attractive" (Patterson, 2003, 1). The ISU is the main sounding-board for professional salvors. The ISU is "an association representing the interest of 46 salvors based in 27 countries and operating worldwide" (ISU, 2005, 1).

In roughly a quarter of a century, ISU salvors have been involved in some 4,500 salvage operations. "The aggregate value of the property salved, ships, cargoes, and bunkers, now amounts to US$26.3 billion (ISU, 2005, 1). In return, ISU salvors received salvage revenue over this period amounting to just over five percent of the total salved values. Every year, ISU salvors recover property valued in excess of US$1 billion; approaching US$1.4 billion in 2001 (Lloyd's Agency, 2005).

Greek ISU member Tsavliris Salvage (International) Ltd. has undertaken an average of about 25 Lloyd's Form salvage operations worldwide each year over the past 50 years. That would total 1,250 salvages, including their extraction of 100,000 tons of oil from the tanker *Eviokos*, which collided with the *Orapin Global* off Singapore in 1997 (ISU, 2005). Tsavliris owns and operates seven large salvage tugs and numerous support craft, covering the Mediterranean, Atlantic and Indian Oceans, east to North Asia. They were instrumental in the arduous six-week salvage of the *Castor*. Because Tsavliris lost US$2.4 million of their *Castor* award, which SCOPIC would have provided them, Tsavliris is now having to seriously reassess their commitment to the market.

With the shift away from property salvage and towards pollution mitigation, "salvage remains an industry under severe financial pressure" (ISU, 2005c). The decline in casualty salvage work is attributed to much stricter vessel and crew safety standards enforced on, and by, flag states, port-state controls, governments, the IMO, P&I Clubs, and classification societies via conventions such as ISM (International Ship Management) Code, SOLAS (Safety of Life at Sea Convention), ITOPF (International Tanker Owners Pollution Federation Limited), who invented the voluntary TOVALOP (Tanker Owner's Voluntary Association to Limit Oil Pollution), and the Oil Pollution Act of 1990 (OPA). "The combination of better electronic navigation systems, more stringent training requirements, international standards for safety, and *severe penalties for marine pollution incidents* has resulted in a fundamental change in the way companies approach salvage, and the way shipowners view salvage" (Patterson, 2003, 1, author's italics).

Drawing on a long history of general maritime law, the standard forms of salvage contract have, to date, been based on the principle of "no cure, no pay;" the heading on all Lloyd's Open Forms (LOFs). This theory is that a salvor who risks their property or lives to save the property or life of another is entitled to a reward, at least for the value of their effort, and often for a percentage of the value of the goods salved as well as pollution damage mitigated. This practice, in use since at least ancient Roman times, has been encapsulated in the LOF since 1892. Lloyd's Open Form provides a regime for deciding the amount of remuneration to be paid to salvage companies, or individual salvors, following the successful salvage of maritime property of any description at sea (Lloyds Agency, 2005, and Patterson, 2003).

Salvage forms currently in use are LOF 2000 and SCOPIC 2000, and Articles 13 and 14 of the 1989 Salvage Convention. Article 14 rewards salvors for mitigating pollution damage even if the vessel is lost. According to the ISU, LOFs are used in most of pure salvage cases (Short, 2003, 1). The LOF 2000 identifies the salvage contractor, the vessel to be salved, whether SCOPIC is incorporated, the place of refuge sought, and the currency and amount to be paid. It has signatures of both the salvor and captain or owner's agent. Most LOF cases are arbitrated at Lloyds Salvage Arbitration in London, U.K.. According to Lloyd's Salvage Arbitrator Ian Short, Esq. (2003), about 60 percent of the cases settle amicably (2003). LOF 2000, enhanced by SCOPIC, seems to be a workable if not a winning combination for today's combined salvage and pollution needs.

The direction of salvage in the future is towards mitigation of pollution damage more than simply rescue of ships, cargo, and sailors. To meet this challenge, shipowners, insurers, and governments need to adapt to new reward schemes, or risk losing the benefits of salvors in times of need. R.R. Churchill and A.V. Lowe address the issue thus:

In the past, delays were often caused when dealing with ships that had suffered accidents and threatened major pollution because of haggling over the terms of the salvage: this was the case with the *Amoco Cadiz* (1978). Such delays sometimes meant that pollution resulting from accidents were worse than would otherwise have been the case. There was no incentive for salvors to take action that could prove beneficial to the environment, unless he could be sure of saving the ship. The 1989 Salvage Convention allows for the salvor to be paid if he prevents or minimizes damage to the environment, even if he does not save the ship (1999, 356).

One of the dedicated ocean-going salvage companies to survive, Les Abeilles, has done so with government backing. "The *Amoco Cadiz* foundered because, in 1978, the French Navy did not have a tug capable of pulling a 500,000-ton oil tanker. The state turned to the private sector, Les Abeilles [and] brought an end to the days when rescue operations were delayed, or, worse, prevented by financial haggling" (Hamon, 2003, 4). This system works because the French government has helped pay for, and subsidize, two salvage tugs at the mouth of the English Channel, 24 hours a day, 365 days a year. The tugs' skippers have authority, via the French Maritime Prefect, to issue a formal demand; "an uncompromising order to put an end to the threat posed to both ship and the environment. [As a result] a distressed vessel is obliged to accept the tug immediately and without bargaining" (Hamon, 2003, 11). Such governmental control over coastwise sea territory was an important but not uniform aspect of both the *Castor* and *Prestige* cases.

To meet this new pollution and regulatory challenge, the ISU, Lloyd's and other underwriters, and national governments, have adopted new, integrated strategies to reward salvors for protecting the environment. The loss of the tanker *Prestige*, like *Castor* before it, illustrates this shift. The governments of Spain,

France, and Portugal refused access to their ports for the disabled, crude-oil-laden ship. Salvage tugs towed the *Prestige* away from land, where it sank. In theory, under Article 14 of the 1989 Salvage Convention, salvors could collect up to 100 percent cost of their efforts, though the ship was lost. In practice, with the *Castor*, this did not prove to be the case, and one third of the award went unpaid. Under SCOPIC, the salvor can collect a tariff amount. This way, insurers and governments pay for the privilege of having salvors lose a ship to save the shoreline, which is exactly what was meant to happen in the *Prestige* case.

The ISU declares that in a growing number of salvage cases, the main priority is to prevent, or at the very least, minimize environmental damage. Pollution defense is now at the top of the agenda (ISU, 2005). In 2001, ISU members salved half a million tons from 247 vessels with pollutant cargoes or bunkers, and in 2000 went to the aid of 310 ships (ISU, 2005). In 2002, ISU members combined to perform 268 salvage operations and saving 957,000 tons of pollutants that would have entered the environment (Patterson, 2003). Significant crude oil spills of over 700 tons are down in volume – from an average of 24 a year in the 1970s to about seven a year in the 1990s. This is a decrease of two thirds, or about 70 percent (ISU, 2005).

The ISU recognizes the priority of protection of the marine environment. Salvors can contract in such a way, by using SCOPIC for example, that they are shielded from loss when responding to high-risk or low-value casualties (ISU, 2005). It turns out that good policy is also good business. The pre-agreed tariff rates of SCOPIC offer a system found preferable to the difficult-to-ascertain value of environmental mitigation. The ISU mission is to 'keep the pollutant in the ship;' once pollutants have escaped from a vessel more than ten percent recovery is rare (Lloyd's Agency, 2005). The ISU concludes that it is now impossible to separate the salvage and pollution defense functions. Environmental defense is now a more critical measure of operational success than pure salvage.

Although SCOPIC only came into law in August 1999, Lloyd's Agency of London has documented nearly 100 cases of its use; 95 salves to October 2003, and 111 to January 2005 (Lloyd's, 2005). Article 14 awards in that times have amounted to roughly US$127 million in salvage awards. One advantage of SCOPIC is that an imminent environmental catastrophe is not required to be proven for the contract to be signed. SCOPIC can serve as a contingency agreement leaving neither party worse off if the anticipated pollution never occurs. This allows owners and salvors to be pro-active in their environmental efforts.

Background Law of Salvage

The law of salvages is as ancient as the law of the sea. Since the laws of Crete, Justinian Roman Law, and Hugo Grotius, any attempt to regulate the sea has crossed many jurisdictional lines, whether between a mother-country and its overseas colonies, or between immediate neighbors who share common coastlines, bays, or riverbanks.

Salvage law exists as one of the sticks in the bundle of laws within the larger corpus of maritime and admiralty law. There are laws to regulate ships, laws to regulate the salvage of ships, and to deem and protect both rewards for salvors and the rights of shipowners. What are needed are laws to protect the rights of coastal states that are victims of the failures of shipowners and salvors, such. "Salvage law has evolved over centuries, and has its origins in antiquity. Laws concerning maritime salvage are found within the Edicts of Rhodes, the laws of the Romans, the Justinian Digest, the Medieval Laws of Oleron, the Code of the Hanseatic Leagues, and were of such significant importance as to be jurisdictionally determined within the Constitution at the founding of the Republic" of the United States (RMS *Republic*, 2000, 1).

"The legal concept that a marine salvor is entitled to a reward for the saving of imperiled marine property has been a

recognized part of the admiralty law for more than 3,000 years"
(SafeSea, 2005, 1). The history of salvage is colorful:

> The Rhodians' maritime accomplishments
> began to reach their height in the late fourth-century
> B.C. The distinguished Rhodian fleet replaced the
> Ptolemaic navy as the enemy of piracy on the high
> seas. Cultures preceding Minoan Crete may have
> recognized a principle of salvors' rights in their
>
> customs and laws (citing Thucydides). The Rhodian
> Sea Law has been dated to about 600-800 A.D., and
> includes provisions awarding 'the fifth part of what
> he saves' to one who saves a ship. The Laws of
> Oleron have been characterized as a foundation of
> the Admiralty Law of England that was signific-
> antly developed by the fourteenth century. This
> ancient rule was followed in U.S. admiralty law,
> and was not altered until 1975 (Gould, 2003, 2-4).

Salvage is still a tough industry. As with army infantrymen,
there are months of rigorous preparation, interspersed with hours
and weeks of tense waiting, punctuated by burst of highly
dangerous non-stop salvage activity. The ISU describes the origins
of salvage thus:

> Marine salvage has a long history. Lloyd's Open
> Form, the industry's famous 'no cure – no pay' contract,
> will reach its centenary in 2008, but the history of
> salvage reaches back many centuries – to the Classical
> World. The divers of Ancient Greece were rewarded
> with a share of property recovered from wrecks. Salvage
> law and practice have evolved over the centuries but the
> central concept, no cure – no pay, remains unchanged to
> this day. In this business, reward is based strictly on
> results.
> The salvor is paid according to the "salved
> value" of property (ships and their cargoes). [He] is free

to choose whether to accept the all-or-nothing gamble.
Success requires the recovery of property, entitling the
salvor to a reward under the principle of 'natural equity.'
Failure, on the other hand, means zero entitlement.
Indeed, the salvor has ample opportunity to lose heavily,
as mobilization for a salvage operation can be
very costly. Salvage expenses tend to be front-end
loaded (ISU, 2004, 1).

Interestingly, the SCOPIC clause which salvors have been
clamoring for goes beyond the simple 'no cure, no pay'
remuneration. SCOPIC stands for the principle that even if the ship
is lost and no property is salvaged, the salvor expects to be fully
paid for pollution prevention. So SCOPIC is altering the paradigm
of salvage in a subtle but distinct way. A salvor operating under
SCOPIC can no longer gripe about 'no cure no pay.' Salvors asked
for pollution remediation rewards whether the ship is lost, and now
they have that option. SCOPIC broadens their options.

The basic principle of rewarding the salvor, but not for
more than the value of the ship and cargo, remained true into the
late 20th century. However, with the advent of mammoth oil
tankers that are capable in a few hours of causing enough
environmental damage to bankrupt most small countries, saving
the ship became less cost-effective. Going into the 21st century,
preventing pollution has become the focus. To recognize this
reality, laws and contracts have had to be changed. One of the most
effective organizations tasked with creating and enforcing uniform
international standards of safety and polity is the International
Maritime Organization, (IMO), formed in 1948 and based in
London, England since opening in 1958.

There are 164 nations (out of roughly 185 total)
participating in, and contributing to, the IMO. Whereas individual
nations can attempt to bring their own port-state-control standards
higher - OPA 1990 followed the *Exxon Valdez*, and recent French
efforts to impose double-hull tankers followed the *Erika* spill - the
most universal maritime regulations are multinational. This is

because shipping is inherently international. Even a domestic oil spill can cross borders. IMO has already, in the space of less than two years following the *Prestige* disaster, implemented two resolutions in 2003 governing Ports of Refuge and Marine Assistance Service (IMO, 2005).

Most of the ship casualties covered in this paper occurred in European waters, and since the most marked reaction to them has been by the European Commission, the Europe-based IMO, and European coastal states, the focus of this paper is European and international shipping law. This is also because the recent spills covered here update the *Exxon Valdez* fallout and resultant legislation, and because when IMO mandates change, it has a higher resonance than when a single country - even the U.S. - does the same, i.e. with OPA 1990. The regulations promulgated on the heels of *Erika*, *Castor*, and *Prestige* represent the leading edge of the regulation of global maritime commerce this century.

Specifically this paper covers maritime case-law governing spills and salvage - from the *Blackwall* case in 1869 to the *Nagasaki Spirit* decision in 1997, as well as government-commissioned reports such as those by the Marine Accident Investigatory Board (MAIB) in the U.K., and government-sponsored report by the likes of Lord Donaldson (1999) and the Comite Maritime International (CMI). Also included are individual European nations' attempts to influence law and policy, as well as attempts by the European Commission manifested in the *Erika* packages (three so far). Finally, there are the recent resolutions made in comity by 164 nations in the IMO; Places of Refuge and Marine Assistance Service.

Another, significant factor in ongoing decision-making is the court of public opinion. This is represented herein by numerous articles by industry mouthpieces, some of them with lobbying slants, and others from the popular press. When dealing with issues of national sovereignty and international cooperation, the results of which could wipe out annual livelihoods for thousands of citizens, the political implications and the power of the press cannot be ignored.

SCOPIC is governed by contract salvage law, which is most often encapsulated under the Lloyd's Open Form contract (Short, 2003). It represents, however, the culmination of a long evolution in general maritime law, and salvage law in particular. SCOPIC can be defined against other areas of law, in order to lay a foundation. Contract salvage and pure salvage differs from the law of finds in that the law of finds deals primarily with abandoned property no longer in peril; i.e. lying on or embedded in the sea-floor or tidal zone. Salvage law must, by definition, include an element of actual peril to either property or limb; in other words a ship adrift or in imminent danger. As the *Prestige* and *Castor* cases illustrate, there was no dearth in either enthralling casualty.

A case which forms the backbone of salvage law involved the casualty of the vessel *Blackwall* in San Francisco in 1867 (The *Blackwall*, 1869). The facts of the *Blackwall* salvage are interesting enough to merit attention here. This is especially so for two reasons: the case demonstrates the exemplary risks assumed by salvors and a strong argument for their remuneration, and the *Blackwall* Test, enumerated by the U.S. Supreme Court, is the bedrock formula of salvage awards, including SCOPIC. That this test's impact is felt throughout the maritime world to this day is demonstrated by numerous salvage awards citing it since. The facts were:

> About four o'clock on the morning of the 24th of August, 1867, the British ship *Blackwall*, then at anchor in the harbor of San Francisco, was discovered to be on fire. Messengers were dispatched to the captain and engineer of the tug *Goliah*, who were asleep at their homes on shore, and every effort made to get steam on the tug as quickly as possible. The captain and engineer were aroused, and at once repaired to the wharf. It being found impracticable for the tug to go into the slip where the fire engines lay, two of the latter were brought around to the wharf where the tug was, and taken across the deck of a steamboat, which lay

between the wharf and the tug, and so [placed] on to the tug with promptitude and skill. About six o'clock the tug, with two engines on board, together with the firemen, etc., attached to them, moved from the wharf, and in a few minutes were alongside the ship

The ship was burning between decks, where the fire first originated. The officers and crew, though assisted by a party from the U.S. ship *Lawrence*, having found all attempts to subdue the flames abortive, had desisted from further efforts, and had. a few moments before the *Goliah* arrived, left the vessel with their effects in small boats. Without speedy assistance the total destruction of the ship and cargo was inevitable. The measures of the firemen and officers of the tug were taken with great skill and energy.

The firemen almost instantly mounted her rails, went thence to her forecastle, and from thence to her deck, sweeping the latter with four powerful streams, by which the fire was speedily controlled. They then descended to her between-decks, and in a little more than half an hour the flames were entirely extinguished. Her anchor was then weighed by the advice of the captain of the tug, and the vessel was towed to certain flats near one of the city's wharves. The tug was then dismissed, and the engines were taken to the shore and landed (The *Blackwall*, 1869, 2-5).

These dramatic events were to have a lasting legal implication, enshrined as the *Blackwall* test, setting the standards on how to reward those who risked all to salve property and prevent damage. Had the *Blackwall* inferno spread, the city of San Francisco might have burned as repeated earthquakes have demonstrated.

In a later case involving the casualty *Mantinia* off Puerto Rico, U.S. District Court Judge Acosta incorporates the elements of the *Blackwall* test into a modern opinion thus:

41

In order to set forth a claim for 'pure salvage,' the plaintiff must establish three elements: 'a marine peril; service voluntarily rendered when not required as an existing duty or from a special contract; success in whole or in part, or service contributing to such success. On the other hand contract salvage is that type of salvage service entered into between the salvors an the owners of an imperiled property, or by their respective representative, pursuant to an agreement, written or oral, fixing the amount of compensation to be paid, whether successful or unsuccessful in the enterprise.

A salvage situation under contract is of two types: (i) it could be for a specific payment which is not dependent upon the success of the rescue, i.e. the amount set by the terms of the contract is owed in any event, or (ii) the contract could be for compensation in an amount which is fixed only after there has been success. The contract in the maritime industry that ties the amount of compensation to the degree of success is the Lloyd's Open Form (Smit, 2003, 120).

Under this opinion, SCOPIC is mostly for a specific payment which is not dependent upon the success of the rescue. There is also a modern recognition that the cost of pollution damage may outweigh the value of the vessel and cargo saved. This is a reflection of the public outcry over the ever-present threat of oil pollution along coastal states.

In U.S. maritime law, six primary circumstances are factored in allowing salvage awards, under either contract or pure salvage law. These are known as the '*Blackwall* test,' since they originated with the *Blackwall* incident described above. They are:

Courts of admiralty usually consider the following circumstances as the main ingredients in determining the amount of the rewarded to be decreed for a salvage service: (1) the labor expended by the salvors in rendering the salvage service; (2) the promptitude, skill, and energy displayed in rendering the service and saving the property; (3) the value of the property employed by the salvors in rendering the service, and the danger to which such property was exposed; (4) the risk incurred by the salvors in securing the property from the impending peril; (5) the value of the property saved; [and]

(6) the degree of danger from which the property was rescued (The *Blackwall*, 1869, 21).

Most, if not all of these enumerated exertions are evidenced in the fact patterns of the *Castor* and *Prestige*. Success was an important, though irrelevant, factor under SCOPIC in the *Prestige* casualty, where it was pre-agreed that, barring negligence, the salvor would be paid whether the ship sank or not. Even after satisfying all of these elements (as in the *Castor*), salvors who have not persuaded vessel owners and their P&I club representatives to sign SCOPIC may be deprived of the award for pollution mitigation. Furthermore, by signing SCOPIC, salvors forego their potential Article 14 award, unless they withdraw from SCOPIC. Signing of SCOPIC must be a pro-active move for it to prevail over all other salvage law except inasmuch as SCOPIC is incorporated into and bound by other terms in the standard LOF. Awards under Article 13 of the Salvage Convention (special compensation) which are higher than SCOPIC prevail.

Contrasting pure and salvage law with SCOPIC, recognized authority Geoffrey Brice, Queen's Counsel had this to say:

The concept of both pure salvage and often contract salvage being governed by the hallowed words 'no cure no pay' is ingrained in both English and American salvage law. If the salvor has carried out the salvage operation in respect of a vessel which by itself or its cargo threatened damage to the environment, and has failed to earn a reward under Article 13 at least equivalent to the special compensation accessible in accordance with this article. Success constitutes a cure, and the value of the property to its owners (not the insurers) at the termination of his services constitutes the fund out of which to reward the salvors. With the ratification of the International Salvage Convention (1989) by the U.S., it would appear that under the constitutional principle of self-executing treaties, Article 13 (1) of the Convention governs the question of assessing salvage remuneration in the U.S., as it does in English law (1999, 1832).

Concerning P&I clubs, Brice further notes that "it is the insurers who pay in respect of salvage services, which include the prevention of pollution damage, even though P&I insurers are liable in the event of pollution damage occurring" (Brice, 1999, 1832).

Professor Mandaraka-Sheppard wrote of SCOPIC that: "the deeming provision of a place of safety, where the service could be terminated, has been clarified by inserting an agreed place of safety in LOF 2000. In practice, salvors have frequently been faced with a situation when local authorities of a port, where the salved property was taken, demanded a large sum of money as a security for alleged or possible contamination of the territorial waters. Clause H (of LOF 2000) is a novel clause which would protect salvors in such situation, by providing for a deemed performance of their services" (2001, 741,745). She quoted Tsavliris Salvage Co. in concluding of the *Castor* affair that:

> It would be a matter of great regret if the *Castor* case were to become a precedent for treating the salvage industry with prejudice or discourtesy whenever it seems expedient to so. It was our belief that the vessel was seen rather as an unwanted political encumbrance. The fact that in a number of instances our detailed salvage plan went unread points to this conclusion. No thanks whatsoever are due to the Mediterranean coastal states that flatly refused to grant the vessel access to sheltered coastal waters, and in the process added significantly to the risks faced by salvage personnel and the environment (Mandaraka-Sheppard, 2002, 743-744).

Speaking of the facts of the *Prestige* shortly after it sank, 14-year IMO President William O'Neil "strongly hinted that he was on the side of those who felt that the stricken oil tanker should have been given a port of refuge when it got into difficulties off the Spanish coast. Had she been given access to sheltered waters, it may have been possible to have transferred the cargo and the effects of pollution could have been minimized. There are clear indications that a *refusal can result in compounding the problem*, which ultimately endangers life, the ship, and the environment" (Osler, 2003, 2, author's italics). Delegates to a similar industry conference discussing the *Prestige* "heard that a key factor raised by the casualty was the need for a clear command-and-control structure, one that was free from political interference." This ideal salvage environment is comparable to the one put forward by Lord Donaldson in his report following the *Sea Empress* spill off Milford Haven, U.K., in 1996 (Osler, 2003, l).

On Tsavliris' loss on appeal of US$2.4 million in the *Castor* case, the ISU president commented that "the nub of the issue is: what constitutes substantial risk to the environment?" He said the ISU was "not happy, globally speaking, that this increment was [reduced] to zero on the grounds that the risk was not substantial" (Lloyd's List, 2002h). On the contentious issue of places of refuge, the ISU has a four-step stance:

> Firstly the ISU wants to see every casualty. The ISU notice that whenever states or local authorities have to give permission for ships to enter their waters, they are advised by 'experts' who have very little knowledge or skill in assessing the risks. The consequences of sending the vessel back to sea must be evaluated and the ISU want to see financial security set at a reasonable level. In the case of France, the decision to give authority to the Prefect Maritime to override decisions taken by port authorities on the issue of refuge is a great improvement (Lloyd's List, 2003, 1).

Since a bunker-spill convention left salvors open to third party claims, the ISU want to push for responder immunity, trying to get agreements in black and white from port states such as those which effectively banished both the *Castor* and *Prestige* - namely Spain, Morocco, Portugal, Algeria, Gibraltar, Tunisia, Cyprus, Malta, and Greece (Lloyd's List, 2002h). Regarding the jurisdiction of SCOPIC, Professor Mandaraka-Sheppard writes:

> Salvage is also a remedy that arises independently of contract [as well as being covered by an arbitration clause] The Admiralty Court has both an inherent jurisdiction to protect the interests of salvors during the course of salvage operations and a statutory jurisdiction under s 20 (2) (j) of the SCA 1981 for any claims under the Salvage Convention, or any contract in relation to salvage services In practice, the salvor's rights to compensation for environmental salvage depends on the cooperation

of the liability insure, the P&I Club, and his right
can be protected by obtaining security for such
claims from the liability insurer. The intention
behind the SCOPIC clause is that such cooperation
will be forthcoming. (2002, 745)

In terms of upper-level cooperation among interested
partied during a casualty, the very existence of the Code of
Practice between the ISU and P&I clubs, plus the cooperation
between classification societies, flag states, and P&I
representatives during *Castor* and *Prestige* indicates some level
cooperation between these participants. In fact, by its very name
SCOPIC is a fusion between the salvors and the P&I interests; the
acronym stands for Special Compensation P&I Club Clause. The
very essence of SCOPIC is to bond salvors; the party which does
the work, takes the physical risks, and has the equipment and
technical skill on the one part, and the P&I Clubs, which negotiate,
contracts for their clients, and ultimately pay, on the other.
Since SCOPIC, and not necessarily LOF 2000, deals
specifically with oil pollution of the marine environment, and since
this is regulated under a different set of laws than just shipping
law, it is helpful to understand the basic tenets of international oil
pollution law. "The most important convention regulating and
preventing marine pollution by ships is the International
Convention for the Prevention of Pollution from Ships, 1973, as
modified by the Protocol of 1978 relating thereto; called
MARPOL, for Marine Pollution. It covers accidental and
operational oil pollution. IMO's so-called Intervention Convention
affirms the right of a coastal state to take measures on the high seas
to prevent, mitigate or eliminate danger to its coastline from a
maritime casualty. The International Convention on Oil Pollution
Preparedness, Response, and Co-operation (OPRC), 1990,
provides a global framework for international co-operation in
combating major incidents or threats of marine pollution" (IMO,
2005).

Articles 13 and 14 of the 1989 International Salvage Convention

Articles 13 and 14 of the 1989 International Salvage Convention, against which SCOPIC has such counterpoint, are salient in the following areas. Article 13 is essentially a repeat of the *Blackwall* (1869) criteria for salvage reward used in American courts. To emphasize this, the word 'environment' is not used once in Article 13. It basically divides the reward among respective salvors equally, on the basis *quantum meruit*; payment on the basis of contribution made. It is Article 14, Special Compensation, which has caused so much consternation in the at least the 22 or so instances that it was invoked since entering effect in 1989 (ISU, 2005). It is noteworthy that Article 14 survived uncompromised by SCOPIC for just over a decade. It has proved overall contentious and very difficult to apply, especially inasmuch as it refers to government compensation. This is a problem, because in cases such as *Prestige* and *Castor*, governments sent the ships away from land to prevent costly spills. The question is, if they have that right, should they not also bear the burden of compensating the salvors?

If SCOPIC fails to fill this jurisdictional void, there may be fewer salvors willing to take the risk to intervene and mitigate environmental damage in the first place, as such exercises and readiness are costly. Item two, Article 14 states that "in no event shall the total increase be more than 100 percent of the expenses incurred by the salvors" (Convention, 1989). There are similarities between the *Blackwall* test and the text of both Articles 13 and 14. Article 13 limits the reward to "not exceed the salved value of the vessel and other property." Article 14 covers salvors only if they fail to receive a reward under Article 13, or alternately that the reward is greater than that available under 13; i.e. if the reward for protecting the environment exceeds the value of the prevention of environmental damage. In the law case In Re *Exxon Valdez* (2001), remedial costs stemming from judgments against the polluter far exceeded the value of the vessel and its cargo either before, during, or after the incident. This case was a good example of this conflicting situation, which both Articles 13 and 14 and SCOPIC sought to re-balance.

Article 13, criteria for fixing the reward, reads as follows:

1. The reward shall be fixed with a view to encouraging salvage operations, taking into account the following criteria without regard to the order in which they are presented below: (a) the salved value of the vessel and other property; (b) the skill and efforts of the salvor in preventing or minimizing damage to the environment; (c) the measure of success obtained by the salvor; (d) the nature and degree of the danger; (e) the skill and efforts of the salvor in salving the vessel, other property and life; (f) the time used and expenses and losses incurred by the salvor; (g) the risk of liability and other risks run by the salvor or their equipment; (h) the promptness of the services rendered; (i) the availability and use of vessels or other equipment intended for salvage operations; and (j) the state of readiness and efficiency of the salvor's equipment and the value thereof.

2. Payment of a reward fixed according to paragraph 1 shall be made by all of the vessel and other property interests in proportion to their respective salved values. However, a State Party may in its national law provide that the payment of a reward has to be made by one of these interests, subject to a right of recourse of this interest against the other interests for their respective shares. Nothing in this article shall prevent any right of defense.

3. The rewards, exclusive of any interest and recoverable legal costs that may be payable thereon, shall not exceed the salved value of the vessel and other property.

Several elements of the *Blackwall* test should be evident to the reader in these criteria.

Article 14 of the Salvage Convention, which is effectively replaced or superseded when SCOPIC applies, reads:

1. If the salvor has carried out salvage operations in respect of a vessel which by itself or its cargo threatened damage to the environment, and has failed to earn a reward under article 13 at least equivalent to the special compensation assessable in accordance with this article, he shall be entitled to special compensation from the owner of that vessel equivalent to his expenses as herein defined.
2. If, in these circumstances, the salvor, by his salvage operations, has prevented or minimized damage to the environment, the special compensation payable by the owner to the salvor may be increased up to a maximum of 30 percent of the expenses incurred by the salvors. However, the tribunal, if it deems it fair and just to do so, and bearing in mind the relevant criteria set out in article 13, may increase such special compensation further, but in no event shall the total increase be more than 100 percent of the expenses incurred by the salvor.
3. Salvor's expenses means the out-of-pocket expenses reasonably incurred by the salvor in the salvage operation, and a fair rate for equipment and personnel actually and reasonably used in the salvage operation.
4. The total special compensation under this article shall be paid only if and to the extent that such compensation is greater than any reward recoverable by the salvor under article 13.
5. If the salvor has been negligent, and has thereby failed to prevent or minimize damage to the environment, he may be deprived of the whole or part of any special compensation due under this article. 6. Nothing in this article shall affect any right of recourse on the part of the owner of the vessel.

SCOPIC 2000 Clause of Lloyd's Open Form (LOF)

Since SCOPIC is incorporated into the Lloyd's Open Form salvage contract, it will be appropriate to understand some of the background and history of the LOF itself, which goes back over a century. Having gone through ten revisions, there are several key dates in its development which are relevant here. Apparently the ISU have been in a kind of partnership with Lloyd's of London Underwriters for a century. This would explain why the ISU has such a say in the LOF; they've been helping to write it since the outset.

The story of LOF began in April 1890, in response to concern regarding the activities of certain salvors in the Dardanelles and Black Sea regions. There had been complaints from Masters of unreasonable behavior by salvors. Invariably, the Master was compelled to sign a contract for payment of a lump sum frequently regarded as grossly excessive. Lloyd's succeeded in persuading [salvors] to agree [to] perform salvage services on the terms of a lump sum contract which, however, gave the Committee or its appointed arbitrator the right to review the agreed figure and to alter it - upwards or downwards - if the figure was considered inappropriate.

It was not until 1907 that Lloyd's and the ISU positions were reconciled. Matters came to a head on June 3, 1907, in the context of a suggestion that "a permanent Court of arbitration" should be established to resolve salvage claims involving Lloyd's and other marine underwriters in London. ...The ISU representatives indicated that they were prepared to disregard the proposal to create an arbitration Court if the standard form of salvage agreement, which Lloyd's were promoting, could be amended to meet their concerns on arbitration (ISU, 2005, 2).

Looking back at the origins of Lloyd's Form, there are parallels with more recent events in the world of salvage. For example, concern that LOF might have become unwieldy was an issue addressed in the production of the streamlined LOF 2000 contract. There are also echoes of the difficult negotiations which led to the SCOPIC agreement. But, as the events show, there remains a willingness to confront these challenges to produce standard forms acceptable to all (ISU 2005, 3).

Like many documents amended by debate, the SCOPIC clause was developed in response to events which seriously undermined confidence in the abilities of its predecessors, Articles 13 and 14 of the Salvage Convention, to satisfy salvor's needs. "These include failure of security, problems of defining the trigger for special compensation; what is a sufficient threat to the environment, what is substantial damage, what are coastal waters, etc., the delay and cost in assessing the uplift in successful cases of pollution-prevention, and in the mechanics of calculating special compensation." (Parry, 1999, 2). As the loss of the *Titanic* proved a catalyst for Safety of Life at Sea and passenger-safety regulations, and as the *Exxon Valdez* spill precipitated OPA 1990 in the U.S., so did the resolution of the <u>*Nagasaki Spirit*</u> litigation under Article 14 galvanize a drafting of SCOPIC. Since the case is so seminal, the basic facts of the casualty follow.

The *Nagasaki Spirit* was a part-laden Aframax crude oil carrier owned by Teekay shipping when it collided with the container ship *Ocean Blessing* in the Straits of Malacca on 19 September 1992. An explosion erupted on the *Nagasaki Spirit*, set both ships and the ocean around them on fire, and killed and all of *Spirit*'s crew except two. 12,000 out of 40,000 tons of the *Nagasaki Spirit*'s cargo spilled into the sea and burned. The fire raged aboard the vessels for a week, until 26 September. The Singapore-based salvage company Semco agreed to salvage both vessels under LOF 1990.

Semco was denied a place of refuge for either ship by the Malaysian government, and preceded to Indonesian waters, where they anchored until 24 October. On that date she shifted to discharge most of her cargo to the tanker *Pacific Diamond* via ship-to-ship transfer (STS). *Nagasaki Spirit* remained in Indonesia until 25 November. Thereafter she was towed to Singapore and surrendered to her owners, afloat, on 12 December 1992. In sum, Indonesia offered the *Nagasaki Spirit* refuge, while Singapore and Malaysia denied it for two months. Only once the ship was no longer a threat did Singapore welcome it. For the purposes of this study, waiting until after refuge is necessary is tantamount to denial of a place of refuge. Similar examples resonate in the case studies section.

Regarding final settlement, the salvor's main complaint was that they were not properly remunerated for their work to limit, and to some extent prevent, worse damage to the marine environment. The analysis of the reward was so dense and complicated that there was a widespread effort to clarify the LOF 1990, with the result that the SCOPIC, Special Compensation P&I Club Clause was born. "Salvors were also concerned by the *Nagasaki Spirit* [decision] that the rates for equipment and personnel cannot include any element of profit. Profit is limited to one uplift, which only applies if damage to the environment is minimized or prevented. The *Nagasaki Spirit* arbitration and the eventual hearing and ruling in the House of Lords were ultimately responsible for bringing about the SCOPIC clause." (Parry, 1999, 3, and Semco, 2005).

Parry notes that the widespread condemnation of the House of Lords' decision in the *Nagasaki Spirit*, which turned the latter into an accounting exercise, reflects that many saw this as the straw that broke the camels back (Parry, 1999, 2, and Semco, 1997). Once SCOPIC became an LOF option in 1999, the very first SCOPIC salvage; of *Arabian Prince* off Djibouti, occurred mid-April of that year (Felsted, 1999). SCOPIC effectively superseded Article 14, on the basis that it must be accepted explicitly, and not implicitly, between owners and salvors. As a result of SCOPIC, Article 14 arbitrations have become a fallback rather than the primary contractual tool. Recent history suggests that, before long, Article 14 will fade into history, as more salvage contractors have invoked special compensation clauses; up from 32 in 2002 to 111 to 2005 (ISU, 2005, and Lloyd's Agency, 2005).

In 2000, substantially reworked editions of the Lloyd's Open Form standard salvage agreement (LOF 2000) and SCOPIC (SCOPIC 2000) became effective. SCOPIC is a clause within LOF 2000, with the Yes/No option included. The LOF standard form is one of the most often used, and easily understood salvage agreements. This is especially true of its 2000 manifestation, which has been simplified to a single sheet of paper. Clause seven of LOF 2000 reads "Is the SCOPIC Clause incorporated into this agreement?" A simple "Yes/No" option is provided. Under the 12-point sub parts to the contract side of LOF 2000, sub-part "C" reads as follows: "Unless the word "No" in Box seven has been deleted, this agreement shall be deemed to have been made on the basis that the SCOPIC Clause is not incorporated and forms no part of this agreement. If the word "No" is deleted in box seven, this shall not of itself be construed as a notice invoking the SCOPIC Clause within the meaning of sub-clause two thereof."

Item B reads "Environmental protection: while performing the salvage services the contractors shall also use their best endeavors to prevent or minimize damage to the environment." This is the crux. Salvors are now expected to expend money and be exposed to protect the environment. SCOPIC is meant to reimburse them for this expense. Does it? Based on 100 or so cases in which SCOPIC has been invoked since its inception, it does (Lloyd's List, 2003, 1). David Hughes (2003, 5), in his article entitled "Salvors want to be paid more for protecting environment," notes that:

> Nowadays there is no doubt that society places great value on natural resources so it stands to reason that society ought to pay handsomely those who put life, limb, and property on the line to save the

environment. The problem is that society does not
pay for such services. Insurers and governments do.
There is no bottomless purse for compensating
salvors.

This very wish has been provided for, as insurers and
owners are required to place US$3 million in an escrow account on
signing SCOPIC in exchange for a 25 percent discount on the final
award (Brice, 1999, and Parry, 1999). SCOPIC is attempting to
ensure that salvors receive their just reward, not just for saving
vessels, which are often beyond much value by the time they are
salved, but for mitigating damage to the environment. As with the
cases of *Nagasaki Spirit, Castor, Exxon Valdez, Prestige*, and *Sea
Empress*, figuring out exactly how to compensate for
environmental mitigation is still a bone of contention. SCOPIC
aims to cure these ills. Whether it succeeds is being played out into
2005.

Specific <u>SCOPIC</u> Clauses

The SCOPIC Clause is actually composed of 15 clauses
and several amendments. It is deemed incorporated into LOF 2000.
If the SCOPIC clause is inconsistent with any other clause, such as
the option of invoking Article 14 of the Convention, it shall, once
invoked, override such other provisions to the extent necessary to
give business efficacy to the agreement. Invoking the SCOPIC
Clause reads: The Contractors shall have the option to invoke by
written notice to the owners of the vessel the SCOPIC Clause set
out hereafter at any time of his choosing, regardless of the
circumstance and, in particular, regardless of whether or not there
is a threat of damage to the environment. The assessment of
SCOPIC remuneration shall commence from the time the written
notice is given to the owners of the vessel and service rendered.
Before the said written notice shall not be remunerated under this

SCOPIC clause at all, but in accordance with Article 13 (SCOPIC, 2000).

Under Item three, security for SCOPIC remuneration, owners are to provide contractor within two working days a bank guarantee or P&I Club letter (called the initial security) in a form reasonably satisfactory to the contractor, providing security for his claim for SCOPIC remuneration in the sum of US$3 million, inclusive of interests and costs. The owner can, however, have the contractor reduce the security to a reasonable sum, and the contractor shall be obliged to do so, once a reasonable sum has been agreed. (SCOPIC, 2000). If the amount is deemed to be higher than US$3 million, the salvors can require a higher security to be paid. Actual final payment amounts are to be arbitrated.

If the owners do not pay security within 48 hours, item four; withdrawal, permits the salvor to withdraw and revert to his rights under Article 14, which shall apply as if SCOPIC clause had not existed. Item five provides tariff rates of personnel, tugs and other craft, portable salvage equipment, out-of-pocket expenses, and bonus due. The contractor is further entitled to a standard bonus of 25 percent of those rates. Item six states that the salvage services under the main agreement (LOF 2000) shall continue to be assessed in accordance with Article 13, even if the contractor has invoked the SCOPIC Clause. However SCOPIC remuneration will be payable only by the owners of the vessel and only to the extent that it exceeds the total Article 13 award. This clause concludes with the salvage award under Article 13 shall not be diminished by reason of the exception to the principle of no cure, no pay (SCOPIC, 2000).

Item seven is of interest; if the SCOPIC Article 13 Award is greater than the assessed SCOPIC remuneration, then the said Article 13 Award shall be discounted by 25 percent of the difference between the Award or settlement and the amount of the SCOPIC remuneration that would have been assessed, had the SCOPIC remuneration provision been invoked on the first day of the services. Item eight concedes that the date for payment will vary according to the circumstances. Salvors are to provide the owners with an indemnity for over payment. Item nine permits the contractor to terminate, by written notice to owners, with a copy to the SCAR (shipowner's casualty representative), if the total cost of his services to date, and the services that will be needed, exceed the sum of a) the value of the property capable of being salved, and b) all sums to which he will be entitled as SCOPIC remuneration. The owners may terminate salvor's service with five days notice, including time of demobilization by the salvors (SCOPIC, 2000).

As far as places of refuge consideration, interference by port authorities and governments are recognized as legitimately adding to demobilization time. Item ten reiterates the salvor's duty to prevent, or minimize, damage to the environment. Item eleven permits owners the sole option of placing their own shipowner's casualty representative aboard the vessel. Lord Donaldson, in his 1999 report, was keen not to have too many representatives swarming over a casualty. This led to the single command- and-control structure headed by the Secretary of State's Representative. The SOSREP has undisputed overall control in the U.K., including over ministers and local groups opposed to providing places of refuge in their euphemistic backyards (Donaldson, 1999).

Item twelve permits P&I Clubs to appoint one special representative, either for hull or cargo, aboard the vessel. Interestingly, such special representatives shall be technical men and *not practicing lawyers* (author's italics). Item thirteen deals with pollution prevention. The assessment of SCOPIC remuneration shall include the prevention of pollution as well as the removal of pollution in the immediate vicinity of the vessel, insofar as this is necessary for the proper execution of the salvage, but not otherwise. Item fourteen deals with general average (GA), distinguishing SCOPIC from general average expenses, except inasmuch as they exceed Article thirteen expenses. GA is excluded from the hull-and-machinery coverage of the vessel. Salvors are to be paid by shipowners, not cargo owners. Finally, Article fifteen states that disputes are to be referred to arbitration as per the main agreement (SCOPIC, 2000).

SCOPIC vs. Articles 13 and 14 of the 1989 Salvage Convention

One of the problems with the pre-LOF 2000 Lloyd's Open Form was that it relied heavily on Articles 13 and 14 of the 1989 Salvage Convention. Clause 14 has since been deemed unworkable in its ability to accurately allocate expenses and costs and rewards for prevention of environmental damage. Yet even LOF 2000 relies on the salvage convention. Sub-part D is subject to the provisions of the International Convention on Salvage 1989, as incorporated into English law relating to special compensation. It is also subject to the SCOPIC clause, if incorporated. The contractor's services shall be rendered and accepted as salvage services, and any salvage remunerations to which the contractors become entitled shall not be diminished by reason of the exception to the principle of no- cure-no pay, in the form of special compensation, or enumeration payable to the contractors under a SCOPIC clause (SCOPIC, 2000).

Another serious concern is the status of places of refuge (IMO, 2005). ISU members insist on ensuring salvors get paid when the focus of the salvors is diverted from vessel salvage to environmental mitigation. As a case study, the *Castor* was towed for six weeks without finding a welcoming port (Lowry, 2002). The *Prestige* sank for lack of permission to approach land. These concerns are being addressed by port-states and the IMO in two resolutions; A.949(23) Places of Refuge, and A.950(23), Maritime Assistance Service (MAS), both adopted in December of 2003 (IMO, 2005).

Summary of ISU, SCOPIC, Salvage Statistics

SCOPIC has applied to 111 casualties since 1999. It is possible that even if invoked, many salvage cases did not actually require the application of SCOPIC, i.e. if no pollution damage occurred or no pollution mitigation was required. Only seven SCOPIC cases have been fully reported between 1999 and 2005

(Lloyd's Agency, 2005). Roughly US$6.8 Million has been awarded under SCOPIC in this time. The ISU reports that for 2001 ISU saved property worth $1.4 billion over 186 LOF cases, which fluctuated from $1 billion to $1.8 from 1991 to 2001 (Seatrends, 2002, 3). In 2003, ISU members salved 218 vessels under LOF, including 303,000 tons in 2003, compared with 603,000 tons of crude oil in 2002. ISU members salved 71,000 tons of bunkers, 160,000 tons of pollutants, including slops and dirty ballast, and 61,000 tons of chemicals (ISU, 2004c).

Figures 3 and 4 (following two pages) show all LOF, Article 13 and 14, and SCOPIC salvage awards published between 1990 and 2004. This information is compiled by the persons and parties who are right at the source; Lloyd's Agency, party of the firm that drafted the first Lloyd's Open Form in consultation with the International Salvage Union in the 1890s. In Figure 3, note the dearth of Appeals since SCOPIC entered force in 1999 (none since 2000). The reader can also compare numbers of LOF contracts to those effectuated under SCOPIC. Figure 4 shows dollar values for salvage jobs undertaken from 1990 to 2004. However, it is not required that salvage awards be published (as far as this author is aware), and so the list, while detailed, is not exhaustive.

				Salvage Awards Published			Article 14/SCOPIC Awards Published		
				Original	Appeal		Original	Appeal	
1990	178		91	51	31	$27,589(77%)	-		-
1991	173		127	63	21	$33,622(76%)	-	-	-
1992	169		105	72	22	$53,825(81%)	2	-	$1,718,373
1993	156		104	58	16	$28,980(58%)	4	-	$707,128
1994	142		110	40	18	$39,633(69%)	3	2	$948,881
1995	121		78	47	25	$36,745(85%)	2	-	$318,633
1996	121		94	24	15	$37,528(85%)	2	2	$1,485,719
1997	104		75	33	16	$24,656(77%)	2+	1	$3,154,183
1998	100		64	30	10	$20,579(83%)	3	1	$1,970,944
1999	123	14	77	30	11	$26,020(84%)	-	2	$2,564,654
2000	133	16	67	22	13	$28,030(77%)	-		-
2001	108	23	82	35	17	$26,904(78%)	3	-	$2,662,876
2002	104	18	55	32	15	$39,422(72%)	1	-	$555,692
2003	89	27	46	29	11	$24,919(84%)	1	-	$1,088,143
2004	91	13	64	35	6	$14,318 (89%)	-	-	-
2005	-	-	-	-	-		-	-	-

* Article 14 Awards/Scopic Awards

+ The Award was for $4,000,000 and was appealed, however, the case was settled before the appeal arbitration was heard. The settlement is believed to have reduced the Award by 4.4%.

FIGURE 3:
SCOPIC SALVAGE AWARDS PUBLISHED, 1990-2004
Source: Lloyd's Agency, (2005c)

The Council of Lloyd's also published 3 Awards relating to Costs which are not included in these statistics.

VALUES ($1,000,000)

Year	Ship	Cargo	Other	Total	% Awards to Values
1990	$284.2	$268.6	$6.9	$559.7	4.9
1991	$277.3	$323.5	$12.5	$613.3	5.5
1992	$389.4	$436.2	$17.8	$843.4	6.4
1993	$150.4	$169.3	$4.0	$323.7	8.9
1994	$119.2	$178.2	$6.7	$304.1	13.0
1995	$193.3	$244.0	$5.6	$442.9	8.3
1996	$182.9	$111.0	$4.2	$295.1	12.5
1997	$169.1	$326.4	$13.0	$508.5	4.8
1998	$101.0	$61.0	$3.8	$165.8	12.5
1999	$53.3	$79.9	$5.8	$139.0	18.8
2000	$61.0	$194.4	$7.5	$262.5	10.7
2001	$50.9	$107.6	$2.5	$161.0	16.7
2002	$81.5	$173.3	$6.6	$264.4	14.2
2003	$72.8	$94.0	$2.3	$169.1	14.7
2004	$47.1	$93.9	$3.9	$144.9	9.9

FIGURE 4:
SALVAGE AWARDS IN U.S. DOLLAR VALUES, 1990-2004
Source: Lloyd's Agency, (2005c)

IMO's Places of Refuge Resolution

The history of the IMO Places of Refuge goes back less than a quarter century. It is clear from the literature that the *Erika*, *Castor* and *Prestige* incidents were catalysts for recent passage of the resolution. As a result of this triumvirate of spills, twenty years of debate were fast-tracked into a resolution in roughly two years. The *Erika* spill occurred on December 2000, *Castor* in 2000 to 2001, and *Prestige* in 2002. The IMO Places of Refuge resolution was passed during December, 2003. Its history is encapsulated thus:

> The notion of providing refuge for ships in distress was raised at IMO during the late 1980s, [during] draft provisions of the International Convention on Salvage (eventually adopted in 1989). Some delegations expressed doubt on the desirability of including such a public-law rule in a private-law convention. It was also pointed out that the interests of coastal states would need to be duly taken into account. Doubt was also expressed whether such a provision would in fact affect the decisions of the authorities of coastal states in specific cases (ISU, 2005, 3-4).

In May of 2001, the IMO recognized that, although the term 'ports of refuge' had been widely used in shipping practice, it did not appear in any of the relevant conventions (e.g. UNCLOS, SOLAS, etc.). Use of the word 'port' might be too narrow and restrictive (IMO, 2005). Thus, the term 'places' of refuge was adopted. A perspective on the catalysts of change in policy by the Europeans (their equivalent of an OPA 1990) is reinforced by then-ISU-President Joop Timmermans' contemporaneous summation:

The effectiveness of response was the issue in 1996, when the tanker *Sea Empress* lost around 70,000 tons of oil in the UK. This led to a comprehensive review of command-and-control arrangements, and the appointment of the SOSREP within the UK's new system of devolved political authority. In late 1999 the *Erika* broke in two off the French coast. This did further damage to the shipping industry's reputation, caused severe environmental damage, and prompted the EU to pursue new regulatory initiatives, the so-called '*Erika* Packages' (ISU, 2004, 5-6).

Article 11, 1989 International Salvage Convention (Places of Refuge)

Article eleven of the 1989 Salvage Convention reads: "A State Party shall, whenever regulating or deciding upon matters relating to salvage operations such as admittance to ports of vessels in distress, or the provision of facilities to salvors, take into account the need for ... preventing damage to the environment in general" (IMO, 2005).

Relevant Excerpts from IMO's Resolution

Definitions 1.18 Ship in need of assistance means a ship in a situation, apart from one requiring rescue of persons on board, that could give rise to loss of the vessel or an environmental or navigational hazard. 1.19 Place of refuge means a place where a ship in need f assistance can take action to enable it to stabilize its condition, reduce the hazards to navigation, and to protect human life and the environment.

Objectives of providing a place of refuge 1.1 Where the safety of life is involved, the provisions of the SAR Convention should be followed. Where a ship is in need of assistance, but safety of life is not involved, [i.e. no *force majeure*] these guidelines should be followed.

1.2 The issue of places of refuge is the solution to a practical problem: What to do when a ship finds itself in serious difficulty or in need of assistance without, however, presenting a risk to the safety of life of persons involved? The best way of preventing damage or pollution from its progressive deterioration would be to lighten its cargo and bunkers and to repair the damage. Such an operation is best carried out in a place of refuge. 1.4 However, to bring such a ship into a place of refuge near a coast may endanger the coastal State, both economically and from the environmental point of view 1.5 While coastal States may be reluctant to accept damaged or disabled ships into their area of responsibility due primarily to the potential for environmental damage, in fact it is rarely possible to deal satisfactorily and effectively with a marine casualty in open sea conditions. 1.6 In some circumstances, [*Prestige*] the longer a damaged ship is forced to remain at the mercy of the elements in the open sea, the greater the risk of the vessel's condition deteriorating or the sea, weather or environmental situation changing and thereby becoming a greater potential hazard. 1.7 Therefore, granting access to a place of refuge could involve a political decision which can only be taken on a case-by-case basis with due consideration given to the *balance* between the advantage for the affected ship and the environment resulting from bringing the ship into a place of refuge, and the risk to the environment resulting from that ship being near the coast.

1.12 The purpose of these Guidelines is to provide Member Governments, shipmasters, companies, and salvors with a framework enabling them to respond effectively and in such a way that, in any given situation, the efforts of the shipmaster and shipping company concerned, and the efforts of the government authorities involved, are complementary. In particular, an attempt has been made to arrive at a common framework for assessing the situation of ships in need of assistance.

1.13 These Guidelines do not address the issue of operations for the rescue of persons at

sea. The safety of persons must nevertheless be constantly borne in mind- if the ship poses a risk [explosion, serious pollution, etc.] to the life of persons in the vicinity [crews of salvage vessels, port workers, inhabitants of the coastal area, etc.]; Is there a possibility of containing any pollution within a compact area? International cooperation? Is there a disaster-relief plan in the area? Evacuation facilities?

1.14 Foreseeable consequences (*including in the media)* of the different scenarios

envisaged with regard to safety of persons and pollution, fire, toxic and explosion risks. Emergency response and follow-up action, such as lightering, pollution-combating, towage, stowage, salvage, and storage (IMO, 2005, 3; author's italics).

CHAPTER 3

METHODOLOGY

Temporal Area of Study

The time period covered in this research is between 1975 and 2005, covering 30 years and roughly 70 places of refuge incidents during that time. The temporal period most carefully studied is the six years between the sinking of the *Erika* off France in 1999 up to the present day. This includes the *Castor* incident in December 2000 to March 2001, the implementation of LOF 2000 and SCOPIC 2000 in 1999, the *Prestige* incident in November 2002, the IMO Places of Refuge Resolution of December 2003, and Spain's Royal Decree of February 2004. The final extraction and tapping of the oil in *Prestige*'s hull did not end until late fall of 2004. Debate about the *Prestige* aftermath and its effect on legislation is ongoing. It will probably continue indefinitely, or until another major oil spill eclipses it.

To the extent that they are relevant, prior maritime casualties, from the *Blackwall* in 1867, *Exxon Valdez* in 1989, *Braer* in 1993, and *Sea Empress* in 1996, are referenced. These historic casualties also contributed to the public's awareness of pollution, and heightened legislators' needs to impose new or improve existing regulations. This study identifies and analyses at least 66 incidents of vessels seeking places of refuge. Each case illustrates an example of ships being either granted or refused refuge by certain countries. Data utilized continues to March and April of 2005 (IMO, 2005), and includes several cases relating to specific hypotheses. While not exhaustive or conclusive, case studies provide a baseline to appraise and test legislation in action.

66

Data Collection

Information has been obtained from organizations whose role is to revise salvage agreements, regulate the shipping industry, track the salvage industry, protect coastal state's shores, and police polluters. These include the Lloyd's Agency Group in London, the International Salvage Union (ISU), the International Maritime Organization (IMO), the European Commission, and the government of Spain. For information on countries which have enforced places of refuge rights, the Comite Maritime International (CMI) has provided an exhaustive report for IMO (CMI, 2002). The IMO itself maintains very thorough databases of topics on point, including the most recent versions of treaties (IMO, 2005). Other data will be obtained from trade and public journals, newspapers, and the world-wide-web, as per the Resources Required section.

Methods of Testing Sub-Hypotheses

H-1) The first sub-hypothesis asserts that to protect the environment, salvors must also be protected financially. Salvors, via the ISU, seek an assurance of profit when their exertions mitigate environmental damage and are not negligent, even if the ship is lost. This will require a two-part analysis. Firstly, Articles 13 and 14 and the relevant Salvage Convention clauses have to be compared closely with SCOPIC. This is done by comparing the two documents clause-for-clause and item-by-item. The process requires mirroring the two documents; taking the relevant material from one document and holding it next to the applicable clause in the other document in order to compare and contrast the two, and see to what degree they overlap, complement, or contradict one another. Then they have to be tested.

The testing occurs by taking the intent of the clauses and testing, to the extent possible, how they pan out in actual casualties. The two most illustrative such casualty cases are the *Prestige* and the *Castor*. In the *Castor* case, the salvor was essentially betrayed by application of Articles 13 and 14. In the *Prestige* case, the salvor was covered and rewarded by SCOPIC.

In this case, extensive analysis of both form and clauses enables the reader to distinguish between the two forms. Since the ultimate purpose of both documents is to enable ship masters and salvors to agree to clear terms of salvage, the SCOPIC form, which is limited to one page of a Lloyd's Open Form agreement, would appear to be the preferable format. By contrast, Articles 13 and 14 were so dense and confusing that it took years for a determination to be made by professional arbitrators in the *Nagasaki Spirit* and *Castor* cases. Initial indicia are that SCOPIC is the superior tool to protect salvors and the environment. The Convention clauses fail for being difficult to comprehend and even more difficult to apply. Ship casualties require instant, informed, and uniform decision-making. SCOPIC is the healthier, clearer younger cousin of the Convention.

Fortunately, there have been at least several opportunities to test the treaties, though not on the scale of the *Erika* and *Prestige* catastrophes which were their progenitors. On one hand are the *Castor* and *Nagasaki Spirit*-type casualties, where the owner has the foresight to opt for the Convention, and chose not to exercise SCOPIC. Now that salvors realize the proven value of SCOPIC, they are more likely to insist on its use in salvage situations involving even the risk of environmental pollution. Parties to the contract can argue in favor of SCOPIC's clarity as well. There is evidence of a serious increase in the use of SCOPIC, and of the near-redundancy in significant incidents of use of the Articles. Since this paper was conceived, more than 100 SCOPIC LOFs have been signed to mitigate against the cost of potential oil pollution. The data available over the past five years, enhanced with examples of places of refuge being denied or granted going back to the mid 1970s, provides a solid enough foundation to both highlight the importance of SCOPIC and also illustrate its predominance in the market. Using comparisons of the outcomes in the *Prestige* and *Castor* incidents will illustrate the ineffectiveness of the Convention, in favor of SCOPIC.

H-2) The second sub-hypothesis, relating to the *Castor* episode, exposed the weaknesses of Articles 13 and 14. To illustrate this, it is worthwhile to follow not only the events of the *Castor* salvage operation, but the wrangling, horse-trading, and promises made during it will be explored. For example, during the *Castor* episode, Spain promised to provide places of refuge in the future (Lloyd's List, 2005, 7). Several countries, including the ship's flag-state, Cyprus, along with Malta, and Algeria, promised places of refuge, which they did not deliver. While the facts alone speak poignantly to the issue, the litigation that followed is even more telling.

The fact that, following the *Castor* case, the salvors had to sue in order to be paid, and the owners, represented by the P&I Club, had to sue to reduce the award, speaks volumes against the party's' decisions to use the Convention instead of SCOPIC. SCOPIC is clear. It is now enshrined in the standard LOF, and it has the advantage of being arbitrated by internationally recognized Lloyd's-appointed Arbitrators. All of these indicators point towards a favorable comparison of SCOPIC over the Convention, both in theory (i.e. clause-by-clause) and in practice; as tested in several relevant casualties.

H-3) The third sub-hypothesis states that IMO's Places of Refuge resolution has the potential to prevent a new *Prestige* incident. Does it? There are compiled data covering almost 70 cases, to choose from in support of or against this sub-hypothesis. Of these, covering 1975 to 2005, only roughly 15 occurred after SCOPIC cover was provided in 1999. Even these provide very telling examples. The container ship MSC *Carla* was refused access to Spain in April 2004 unless it posted Euro $1 million bond, even though the ship was not a tanker and was not leaking. Yet, in June 2004, the LPG tanker *Henrietta Kosan* was rescued by Spanish tugs without penalty. The inconsistencies between these cases are glaring. The message is clear; IMO resolution or not, Spain and coastal states can do as they wish. The evidence and conclusions drawn from the catalogue of incidents suggests that coastal states, and not shipowners, captains, and salvage masters, are in the driver's seat when it comes to whether or not a ship can seek places of refuge along coastal states. Even the time-honored exception for *force majeure* appears to have fallen to this now customary practice.

H-4) The fourth sub-hypothesis states that the *Erika*, *Castor*, and *Prestige* incidents, taken together, have been the impetus for most recent European maritime legislation. The *Titanic* disaster in 1912 led to SOLAS. The *Torrey Canyon* spill of 1967 led to the Cargo Liability Convention (CLC). The *Exxon Valdez* spill in 1989 led to OPA 1990, and the *Erika* Packages led indirectly to single-hulled tankers being phased out from Europe faster than they have been in the U.S.. Taken together, the *Erika*, *Castor*, and *Prestige* casualties and their fallout may have been seminal in spurring and guiding European and international maritime policy since 1999. *Erika* was offered a place of refuge, however the old ship could not withstand the beating. *Castor* was castigated by several coastal states, yet she survived days of force 12 gales. Her salvage saga illustrates just how unwelcoming port states can be. The *Prestige*, through terrible mismanagement by Spain, showed the underbelly and fallibility of coastal states as well as the need for places of refuge legislation. The question of whether any of this has really, pragmatically, changed the regulatory landscape is open.

These three recent accidents certainly changed the political landscape. Because of the unique circumstances of any casualties, even those, like these, that suffered no human fatalities, the incidents also show the difficulty of legislating around a single event. Evidence of the influence of these three mishaps on European internal and international politics, as well as on international outcry and legislative amendment, is on the record. The challenge will be to prove a sufficient nexus, not between these three casualties and newly-minted legislation, but to apply that legislation to mishaps which have yet to occur. The fact that *Erika*, *Castor* and *Prestige* were in their own way unique mishaps means that legislation covering all three is thus able to cast a somewhat larger net in terms of the breadth and scope of the incidents intended to be encompassed.

H-5) The fifth sub-hypothesis is proposed to verify whether it can be reliably predicted which countries will offer places of refuge in the future. As part of improving IMO's Places of Refuge resolution, coastal states should publish lists of available places, despite the potential political challenges. Doing so will reliably identify places of refuge and tilt the balance of enforceability from coastal states to the IMO.

It is asserted that, because of the unique nature of each incident, predicting how specific coastal states will respond to particular casualties is exceedingly difficult to project. However, extrapolation may be attempted based on coastal states' past behavior in order to try to see if they have been inconsistent before, and if so, why? Data informs as to whether coastal states have so far actually granted refuge, denied ships refuge or, possibly, done both. The number of incidents of denial versus rejection should also be telling. However these data merely permits informed conjecture based on past responses. It does not accurately predict future behavior. The highly individualized and unpredictable nature of major oil-tanker casualties makes this analysis more challenging, particularly when speculating about the future.

H-6) The sixth sub-hypothesis states that the IMO's Places of Refuge was meant to outweigh, or trump, Spain's Royal Decree. It is asserted that the intent of the IMO's Places of Refuge Resolution was to increase the sense of obligation of coastal states to offer places of refuge. This may be true even if only by virtue of the force of numbers; those 111 states acceding to the resolution. Coastal states are meant to recognize and act upon when faced with casualties such as *Erika*, *Castor*, and *Prestige*. The intent of IMO and its supporters (ISU, P&I Clubs) was to pressure coastal states into adopting the resolution and complying with the spirit of its principles. The ultimate goal of the resolution is to soften the coastal states' hard resistance to accepting disabled casualties and foster a sense of duty-bound cooperation with parties interested in the outcome from the vessel's, not the coastal state's, perspective.

While the places of refuge resolution is an important step towards meaningful, enforceable consensus, and assuages shipowners who are having to cope with losing the benefits of *force majeure* as a traditional crutch, it does not match the royal decree in terms of enforceability. Since this is really the ultimate question of the paper, all available inputs and informational tabulations of refuge, both denied and granted, to support the original hypothesis in favor of the IMO resolution. Tabulation of actual places of refuge incidences since 1975 suggest that coastal states are going to permit, or deny, ships based on their own internal methodologies, and not because IMO, or any other party, requests they do. This applies even to member states which are signatory to the IMO Convention; 165 of the 184 countries (roughly one third of all nations) worldwide. Because analysis of this sub-hypothetical speaks to the hypothesis of the paper overall, it will also be dealt with in the analyses sections.

Delimitations

Several delimitations are necessary to better define the scope and limitations of this paper. One way to achieve focus is to define what the paper is by what it is not.

1) This paper does not propose to conclude the exact causes of the *Prestige*, *Castor*, *Erika* or other shipwrecks. The paper deals with consequences more than causes.

2) This paper does not propose to allocate blame to specific governments, organizations, Masters, sailors, owners or ship operators for any of the casualties. The purpose of the paper is to analyze decisions and actions of various individuals and groups, in order to determine and, where possible, anticipate the best way forward.

3) This paper is not industry-sponsored, and does not purport to exonerate any individual or industry, organization or its

representatives. Inasmuch as the salvage industry, as well as P&I clubs and governments, are required to work together to resolve, abate or prevent environmental damage, their roles are discussed. To the extent that these parties' actions are effective, they receive due credit.

4) This is not strictly a law paper. Its purpose is to examine the effects of specific oil spill casualties in the context of the evolving understanding of their effects and implications. Inasmuch as these casualties contribute to the amending and creation of laws, the two corpus (casualties and legislation) intertwine and are relevant together.

5) This is not a history paper. It is not intended to cover all of the vessel casualties which influenced various legislative amendments and case decisions. That being said, the list of places of refuge incidents 1975-2005 can be considered one of the most comprehensive available, since it results from every IMO member country's contributions to a formal Comite Maritime International questionnaire prepared for the IMO (CMI, 2002), despite that glaring gaps of enumerated countries, namely Japan, China, India, Russia/U.S.S.R., and India.

The primary cases considered (*Castor* and *Prestige*) are still open for analysis. Except possibly as regards the settlements in the *Castor* casualty, there are no known final figures at this time for the full environmental payout for the *Prestige* incident. Estimates range from 1.5 billion Euros (Tyler, 2004) to 5 billion Euros (WWF, 2003). Even the *Exxon Valdez* costs are to some extent ongoing, with the legal cases not being finalized until over a decade following the actual spill (In Re *Exxon Valdez*, 2001).

6) In terms of time and place, data is collected from places of refuge incidents worldwide between 1975 and 2005. The specific focus of the paper is on northern Europe between 1999 and 2005. The *Erika, Castor*, and *Prestige* incidents all occurred in northern Europe, and the Bay of Biscay, Mediterranean Sea. The chronological period is between the *Erika* spill in 1999, up to Spain's Royal Decree of February 2004. Fallout from, and clean up of, the *Prestige* spill is ongoing to early 2005. Put succinctly, this paper focuses on European and international shipping law in the

73

first half-decade of the 21st century, with a particular emphasis on oil tanker spills and places of refuge in northern Europe during this time.

Resources Required

The primary sources of information on the status and testing of SCOPIC and the IMO Places of Refuge are found in original documents promulgated by Lloyd's of London (LOF), and the IMO; Places of Refuge resolution with explanatory text. The ten primary categories of resources are:

1) Original documents from quasi-governmental (IMO is a subsidiary of the UN), including the text of several international agreements and surveys. This includes minutes and keynote speeches from delegations leading up to passage and debate of legislation.

2) Case studies of individual mishaps as discussed in both the popular press and trade publications (Fairplay, Tradewinds, Lloyd's List, etc.). Research to compile the list of incidents involved searching databases maintained by the ITOPF, CMI, and IMO et al.

3) Academic commentary from established texts on international and maritime law such as Churchill & Lowe (1999), Brice (1999), and Mandaraka-Sheppard, (2002).

4) Actual maritime law cases with relevant law (*Exxon Valdez, Nagasaki Spirit, Blackwall, Smit*, etc.), some of them stretching back 130 years.

5) Email correspondence between the author and several industry participants, including representatives of Lloyd's of London Arbitration Branch, shipowners, and salvage industry participants. Furthermore, the author has had numerous in-person discussions with market participants at industry functions such as the annual Connecticut Maritime Association (CMA) shipping conferences, held in the end of March each year, including 2003, 2004, and 2005, and Propeller Clubs circulars.

6) Analysis from ship casualty reports (LloydsAgency.com) of vessels which have been denied or

granted places of refuge in the past five years. The purpose is to show both successful and unsuccessful places of refuge bids, and, where possible, to show pollution damage and whether there was remediation or prevention of pollution.

7) Analysis of IMO's Further Reading for data and press reports on casualties.

8) Data from the ISU (marine-salvage.com) showing, how many tons of pollution were salved, and what the salvors' rewards were, in net and gross forms. Lloyd's Agency provides exactly how many successful SCOPIC cases were invoked.

9) Data from ISU site on how much the salvage industry has earned under SCOPIC. This is key since when the research was begun in 2003, there was only one SCOPIC case. Since then, tracking the burgeoning number of SCOPIC LOFs is easier.

10) Also, basic information for case study research from an exhaustive survey of over 100 IMO-member states regarding their history of granting or denying places of refuge (CMI, 2002). Out of about 70 places of refuge case studies found, the author independently researched roughly the first 20, and found most of the balance in the CMI Report. The Further Reading section of this paper is 25 pages long and contains some 300 articles, governmental, scholarly and general- media articles. It is an excellent resource (IMO, 2005c).

To this end, the bibliography contains some 150 citations in 11 pages, which have been studied and gathered over more than two years. The worldwide web and internet resources have been scoured, particularly as regards actual events of the *Prestige* and *Castor* incidents. While representing only a small percentage of bibliographic citations, the web has been instrumental in providing detailed casualty reports on these casualties. The internet saved substantial time and money, since otherwise documents and data would have had to have been purchased and mailed from London, England. Because both *Castor* and *Prestige* were covered under LOF salvage agreements (the *Erika* was not), Lloyd's Agency of London keeps a careful tabulation of all relevant articles which were published by Lloyd's List International, the marquee daily report. This has provided invaluable information. LOF 2000 and SCOPIC 2000, as well as the Donaldson Reports and all applicable IMO resolutions are easily available online and to the public.

For access to detailed articles on SCOPIC, search-engines such as Lexis Nexis and Westlaw provided the original texts for numerous legal cases, e.g.; *Exxon Valdez, Blackwall*, and *Nagasaki Spirit*). The University of Rhode Island (URI) library catalogues, HELIN and other databases have been scoured. The following library collections have been physically visited and referenced; Newport, RI, Public Library , Boston Public Library, URI Kingston's Main Library and Marine Affairs Department (periodicals and trade publications), the Roger Williams University School of Law Library, the Boston Public Library, including Copley and Charlestown, the Boston Athenaeum, the Bunker Hill Community College Library, Charlestown, Massachusetts, and libraries of the Massachusetts Institute of Technology (MIT), including the Hart Nautical Museum of the Center for Ocean Engineering, Cambridge, Massachusetts.

A primary task of the paper is to synthesize these various and differing resources. In order to understand and apply SCOPIC to specific cases, attention must be given to its actual text and relevant parts. Therefore, several pages are devoted to a detailed analysis of Articles 13 and 14 of the 1989 Salvage Convention and to LOF 2000, SCOPIC 2000. The major goals of the paper are to better understand the primary documents at issue (LOF and IMO resolutions), to review the basic law of salvage as it has applied pre- and post-LOF 2000, to provide a sense of public policy considerations as illustrated in the popular and industry press, and to generate a synthesis of all three resources into actual revised legislation, namely the Places of Refuge Resolution, France's *Erika* Packages, and Spain's Royal Decree.

While the *Castor* case made it to arbitration and has been to a large extent fully litigated, the *Prestige* incident has not yet led to major legal cases of the type that can be seen as conclusive regarding liability and costs apportionment. The IMO Resolution has thus moved relevant law further and faster than the courts of law have been able to. In order to understand this, it is worth considering that the final, conclusive cases emanating from the 1989 *Exxon Valdez* spill were not issued until 2001, some twelve years after the event. It will probably be another decade until all aspects of the *Prestige* damages have been litigated, arbitrated, or settled, even bearing in mind that in general the European citizenry are far less litigious than their counterparts in the United States. For this reason, the IMO Resolution, inasmuch as it was almost certainly influenced by both the *Castor* and *Prestige* incidents, as well as the *Erika* disaster, is the latest resource applicable to an understanding of the effects of each spill.

The specific resources referred to are carefully cited alphabetically in the bibliography using author, date, title and publisher, and are referenced in the text citing author, date, and, where applicable, page. A list of Further Reading provides 25 pages of articles from all sources which are on-point to the Places of Refuge Resolution.

Assumptions

Before the research proceeded, the following assumptions have been made:

A-1) It is assumed that the exact cause of the initial rupture of the *Prestige'*s hull is not known. The spill, and not its initial causes, are the focus of this research.

A-2) It is assumed that had the *Prestige* been towed towards shore and into a sheltered cove or harbor along the Galician coast of Spain, that substantially less oil would have emitted from the hull, and that the coasts of France and Portugal would have been only nominally effected. The oil did not spill until after the ship was turned away.

A-3) It is assumed that, had the *Prestige* been fitted with double-hulled tanks, emission of oil would have been nil to negligible, permitting the ship to enter a place of refuge for repairs without the concomitant political fallout and spotlight.

A-4) It is assumed that the IMO Places of Refuge Resolution will stand, and that it will not be tested by an actual major pollution incident in the course of this paper.

A-5) It is assumed that had the first coastal states Morocco and Spain, permitted *Castor* to bunker off their coasts, that other countries in the Mediterranean Sea would also have been more receptive to offering a port of refuge to the ship.

CHAPTER 4

CASE STUDIES OVERVIEW

Places of Refuge Data 1975-2005: Denied or Granted

In order to test the hypothesis and sub-hypotheses regarding how coastal states are meant to and actually do react to ships in need of assistance off their shores, it is asserted that as many sample incidents of vessels seeking places of refuge would be highly informative on the issue. With this in mind, considerable attention has been focused on gleaning as many actual places of refuge incidents as possible.

The two resources which have been most helpful have been the IMO's Selected Reading list concerning their Places of Refuge Resolution. The 300 or more citations covering 25 pages are invaluable research tools, and revealed 17 verifiable places of refuge instances since the early 1990s (IMO, 2005). Other helpful resources were annual reports, following the much-discussed *Erika, Castor*, and *Prestige* cases, by the International Union of Marine Underwriters (IUMI, 2001, and Prebble, 2001), and keynote speakers at other conferences (Murray, 2005, OCIMF, 1981, Lacey, 2004). Organizations which monitor oil spills generally provide helpful data summaries (ITOPF, 2005, and CEDRE, 2005).

The second tool which has been invaluable has been discovery of a report undertaken by the Comite Maritime International of Paris, and submitted to the IMO's Marine Safety Committee (MSC) in 2002. The report focuses on the Places of Refuge issue. Furthermore, the authors have initiated a questionnaire to gather raw data from each individual member of the 165 nations signatory to the IMO Conventions. While there are several gaps in responses from important maritime nations such as China, Russia/former U.S.S.R., India, and Japan.

While this survey is not definitive, it does represent at least 66 actual places of refuge instances worldwide over more than 30 years. Forty two coastal states are featured, the breakdown of individual countries appearing in Table 1. Several inconsistencies and statements appended to the CMI survey (2002) are worth noting. For casualties which occurred in higher latitudes, the vast majority happened in the middle of winter. According to the Plimsoll system of loadlines, WNA, or Winter North Atlantic. represents some of the most fearsome and deadly weather known to mariners. This is particularly true in the Bay of Biscay, where the *Erika* and *Prestige* hull failures occurred. It is significant that a majority of these casualties occurred during winter months and in particularly hostile bodies of water, including the Maritime Provinces of Canada, the Southern Ocean off of Australia, and South Africa's notoriously rugged coastline. A dearth of natural harbors added to hostile weather and the heavy shipping traffic in these areas makes the issue of refuge all the more important in these regions.

In terms of participants in the survey, several comments were noteworthy. In answering which countries had offered places of refuge to ships in distress, four countries responded that yes, they had, yet they do not appear under the 'granted refuge' survey in this study. Those countries are Germany, Greece, Japan and South Africa, which claimed to have granted refuge to 30 vessels, though this study attributes only one case, the *Sun*, to South Africa. Japan states that they would offer refuge given the seamanlike option. Hong Kong claims not to have offered refuge, though this study credits them twice. Germany and Greece respond with vague assurances that they offer refuge; Greece used the word 'often' to describe how many times it had offered refuge, though they denied *Castor* during her time of greatest need. Three countries made a point of saying they had never had such refuge vessels at their mercy. They are Argentina, Denmark, and Chile, which suffered the 54,000-ton *Metula* spill in 1974 (ITOPF, 2005).

On the side of coastal states having never denied places of refuge, the same three countries (Argentina, Chile, and Denmark), are joined by France, Germany, Greece, Hong Kong, and Sweden. This is unusual only inasmuch as, according to research, France has joined other countries like its neighbor Spain and also

Portugal, in at least three rejections, including the *Prestige*, *Ya Mawlaya*, 1994, *Andros Patria*, 1978, and several more damaging spills in which France was but one of several countries doing the rejecting. Notably, Greece denied the Greek-owned *Castor* until it had been fully emptied of cargo after six weeks in tow during early 2001. Germany accuses Denmark of having denied refuge to a ship, resulting in the ship washing ashore in Germany. Research indicates consistency with Hong Kong and Sweden's claims not to have denied refuge.

As a final note, several vessels, such as *Alnar* in 2001, were rejected by several countries (Benin, Togo, Ghana), but welcomed by one (Nigeria), or the other way around. Rather than repeat individual vessels, the *Alnar* was shown as having been granted refuge, and all four countries were tallied according to their response; Benin, Togo, Ghana as one denial each, Nigeria with one acceptance. Because of its importance as a legal case, only Nagasaki Spirit is featured on both the 'denied' and 'granted' columns.

The following compendium of truncated case-studies should be allowed to speak for itself. The focus of the summary at the end is not on the vessels, as no vessel was repeated in the research, nor on the length of time denied refuge (an interesting factor unnecessary to this study). The focus of this study is on the behavior of coastal states to different sets of casualties over more than a quarter of a century.

Vessels Denied Refuge: Twenty-six Case Studies

1) *Attican Unity*. This ship suffered a fire and was refused entry to Belgium in 1977 (CMI, 2002).
2) *Christos Bitas*. A tanker laden with 35,000 tons of crude oil, on 12 October 1978 the ship hit bottom while *enroute* up the St. George's Channel, between England and Ireland, but continued its passage. When oil was detected fouling the wake, the vessel was stopped, the crew evacuated, and a ship and cargo salvage

team took over. The British SOSREP (Secretary of State's Representative) ordered the ship, after seven days of ship-to-ship (STS) lightering operations, to be towed to a deep water spot off Ireland for scuttling. In deteriorating weather, the ship was abandoned and sank *enroute* to the scuttling site (CMI, 2002).

3) *Andros Patria*. A tanker of 208,000 tons, built in 1970, suffered an explosion due to a large leak in its hull, while carrying Iranian heavy crude oil off of Spain's Cape Finisterre on December 31st 1978. Thirty-four of the crew-members were killed in the resulting fire, and roughly 60,000 tons of crude were lost in the ocean. A salvage team boarded *Andros Patria* on 4 January 1979, after the three surviving crew had been evacuated. The governments of Portugal, Spain, France and Britain refused the ship permission to enter their territorial waters. Salvors towed the tanker to within 250 miles south of the Azores Islands, Portugal. By 9 February, the convoy was 200 miles northwest of Spain's Cape Verde Islands, off Africa. On 19th February, the government of Portugal permitted the ship to approach its coast, and she berthed in Lisbon that day. Ultimately, *Andros Patria* was sold to Spanish breakers for scrap (CMI, 2002).

4) *Aeolian Sky*. A Greek-flagged general cargo ship of 14,385 gross tons (GT), it was involved in a collision with the coaster *Anna Knuppel* in the English Channel on 3 November, 1979. The tug *Abeille Languedoc* took the ship under tow, however the Port Authorities of Southampton and Portsmouth, U.K., refused her entry. On 4th November, while under tow in gale conditions off the coast of England, the *Aeolian Sky* sank with full cargo (CMI, 2002).

5) *Prinsendam*. A passenger ship under tow by salvage tugs. On October, 1980, the United States government reportedly refused this ship access to the smoother Inside Passage, along the Gulf of Alaska (CMI, 2002).

6) *Khian Sea*. A Liberian-registered ash barge, which left Philadelphia, US, on September 5th, 1986, carrying 14,000 tons of incinerated garbage from the Roxborough incinerator there. During the next two years, the ship was denied entry to Bahamas,

Bermuda, Dominican Republic, Honduras, Guinea-Bissau, Senegal, Cape Verde, and Netherlands Antilles. Haiti permitted it to discharge 4,000 tons, then ordered it to reload and had the navy force the barge out. Later Sri Lanka and Indonesia turned the ship away. In August, 1998, *Khian Sea* was renamed *Felicia* and visited Yugoslavia for repairs. In November of 1988 the *Felicia* arrived at Singapore *enroute* between Suez and Philippines, without any ash, which was reportedly dumped into the Indian Ocean along the way (Greenpeace, 2004, and Hayward, 2002).

      7) *Mobro 4000.* This garbage barge and its escort, the tug *Break of Day,* left New York on March 22, 1987, laden with 3,200 tons of trash. During the next six months, the duo traveled 6,000 miles along the U.S. eastern seaboard, the Gulf of Mexico, and the Yucatan peninsula, off Mexico. Its cargo was rejected by several states in the U.S., then by the governments of Mexico, Belize, and the Bahamas. In October, the trash was converted to 430 tons of ash, and buried in Islip, New York (News of the Odd, 2004).

      8) *Khark 5.* A ULCC (Ultra Large Crude Carrier) tanker, carrying 250,000 tons of Iranian crude oil between Kharg Island and Europort, the ship experienced several explosions while transiting off the coast of Morocco on 19th December, 1989. Abandoned, the ship blazed for three days until a *Smit-Tak* tug could secure it. Spain and Morocco refused salvors' requests for places of refuge. As a result, between 40,000 and 60,000 tons of oil escaped into the sea. The ship was further denied access to the waters of the Canary Islands, controlled by Spain, and the Madeira Islands, controlled by Portugal. Senegal and the Cape Verde Islands likewise banned the *Khark 5.* After roughly six weeks, the ship was able to transfer some of its cargo via ship-to-ship operations roughly 250 miles west of Sierra Leone. Ultimately the ship steamed to Greece, where it was repaired (CMI, 2002).

      9) *Toledo.* In 1990, this ship was under salvage tow when the Minister of Marine for Ireland ordered the salvors not to bring the vessel into Ireland's territorial waters (CMI, 2002).

      10) *Protokletas.* A Greek-flagged Panamax bulk carrier laden with iron ore. During a voyage to Brazil in 1992, the crew

heard the sound of the ship's structure failing and made for the port of Angra Dos Rias, where the ship was denied entry by the Port Authority. The ship spent nine months awaiting permission to enter port to part-discharge her cargo and effectuate repairs, but permission was never given. Unable to find refuge, the vessels' owners ultimately took the ship to deep water and scuttled not only the ship, but its cargo, resulting in total loss of both (CMI, 2002).

11) *Aida*. Another vessel denied access to Brazil by naval authorities in light of her perceived unsafe condition. No further details. Brazil's report to CMI (CMI, 2002).

12) *Long Lin*. In 1992, this ship was refused entry to Belgium after experiencing collision damage (CMI, 2002).

13) *Nagasaki Spirit*. An Aframax crude-oil carrier, which collided with the container ship *Ocean Blessing*, in the straits of Malacca, on 19th September 1992. An explosion which killed all but two of the crew ensued. Semco salvors towed the ship towards both Malaysia and Singapore, but were denied places of refuge, eventually settling on an anchorage off Indonesia. After two months of STS operations, on 25 November, *Nagasaki Spirit* was towed to Singapore and returned to her owners, Teekay Shipping (Semco, 1997). Singapore denied refuge for as long as it was truly necessary.

14) *Ya Mawlaya*. A 50,000-ton bulk-carrying ship, laden with soyabeans, was involved in a collision with the 135,000-deadweight (DWT) laden tanker *New World* off the coast of Portugal, on 21 December, 1994. There were explosions and a fire and eight crewmen were killed. Spain, France and Portugal refused to allow the ship access to their ports except for Valencia. The conditions of refuge offered at Valencia were too strict to attract the owners. The owners signed a Lloyd's Open Form 2000 with salvors. Unable to transfer cargo in a place of refuge, the *Ya Mawlaya* lightered while under tow; a risky and difficult operation. The ship was towed to Malta for repairs (CMI, 2002).

15) *Iron Baron*. In 1995, this laden bulk-carrier grounded on a reef off southern Australia. The Australian government refused the ship access to Launceston to discharge its cargo. The

Tasmanian Government likewise refused a request by the ship to lighter in the lee of Flinders Island (CMI, 2002).

16) *Smirdan*. A Romanian-flagged, general-cargo ship carrying cold-rolled steel coils and soyabean meal between India and the Far East. In January, 1997, the ship ran aground in the Malacca Straits, Southeast Asia. Under a LOF the ship was towed to Singapore, where the Port of Singapore Authority denied the ship access unless the owners posted a bond of US$10 million. Owners were unable, or unwilling, to pay the bond. The ship lay at anchor outside Singapore for three years. After this time the cargo, insured for US$2 million, was sold as part of a settlement for US$25,000 (CMI, 2002).

17) *Ventura*. A tanker carrying molasses between India and Korea, the *Ventura* began to experience structural problems off the coast of Sri Lanka during 1999. Denied access to the port of Colombo, the ship lay disabled at anchor outside the port for four weeks. When the monsoon arrived, the ship broke up while at anchor. Ship and cargo, valued at roughly US$2 million were total losses (CMI, 2002).

18) *Castor*. Oil product-tanker stricken with a cracked hull and egress of gasoline cargo off Nador, Morocco, late December 2000. The ship was denied access to Morocco, Spain, Tunisia, Algeria, Malta, Gibraltar, Greece and Cyprus until after the STS operation was completed in open water. In early February, 2001 *Castor* discharged its balance 23,000 tons cargo to tanker *Yapi* via STS roughly 100 miles from Tunisia. *Castor* was ultimately towed to dry-dock in Greece on 16 February (Lloyd's Agency, 2005).

19) *Treasure*. A bulk-ore carrier, sank off Cape Town, South Africa, in late-June 2000, spilling 400 tons of bunkers. Previously 900 tons of bunkers were vacuumed out. The South African government forced the ship from its berth under threat of an assault from helicopter to commandeer the ship. The crew were evacuated, and a tow attached. However, in the strong winds the tow broke after the ship was towed from Cape Town. The ship broke up after drifting ashore. These facts are very similar to those of the *Prestige* in 2002 (Lloyd's Ship Manager, 2000, 5).

20) *Sea (Ex-Regent Sea).* A 778-passenger cruise ship, built in 1956 as *Gripsholm,* while named *Sea,* she was under tow by the tug *Simoon enroute* to breakers in India when she sank off South Africa. Port authorities in Algoa Bay (about 83 miles south southwest of Cape Recife) refused entry to the disabled ship, which had a 30-degree list and was hove to in a storm. They feared pollution from her 60 tons of gasoil bunkers. Disabled on the 6th, the ship sank on 16 July, 2001. *Sea* had been under tow between Tampa, Florida and India, and was rifled by pirates off Dakar, Senegal (Lloyd's List, 2001g).

21) *Tampa.* A Norwegian-flagged container ship carrying over 438 Afghan, Iraqi and Palestinian refugees rescued from a sinking Indonesian boat used by smugglers. *Tampa* was denied access to Australia's Christmas Islands on Aug. 26, 2001. *Tampa* was delayed three days waiting off the island. The captain feared that his unwelcome, hungry and human cargo, forced to wait on the hot deck, would either deplete the ship's food supply or mutiny. They outnumbered the ship's crew significantly. When the *Tampa*'s Master defied the Australians and attempted to approach the island, Australian special forces intercepted and boarded the ship. Later, the refugees were transferred to an Australian Navy ship and taken to Nauru, in the Pacific Ocean. *Tampa* then resumed her voyage. The delay was particularly frustrating since the Australian navy initially vectored the *Tampa* to the rescue, then ordered the ship to more distant Indonesian islands. A national election in Australia, in which toughness on immigration was a platform, was imminent and considered a factor in Australia's behavior (Penelope, 2002, 1).

22) *Bismihita'La.* A 15,434 DWT Liberian general-cargo ship was disabled some 500 miles west of South Africa on 30 August, 2001, after developing cracks in the hull and a 30-degree list. Over two weeks the ship was denied access to both South African and Namibian ports. Three of the Indian crew in a liferaft were struck by the ship's propellers and killed during rescue attempts. Taken under tow by *Smit Pentow,* the P&I Club, and underwriters decided to scuttle the ship, as no viable ports would

accept it. On 17 September, 2001 the *Bismihita'La* was scuttled professionally, roughly 200 miles off the coast of Namibia (CMI, 2002).

23) *Ikan Tanda*, A Singapore-flagged 10,000-ton bulk carrier, ran aground off Scarborough, South Africa, on 5th September, 2001, laden with fertilizer. Though *Smit Pentow* salvors were able to tow the ship from the rocks, where she ran aground after her engines flooded in a storm, the South African Marine Safety Authority (SAMSA) denied the ship access to any ports in the country. The ship was towed 200 miles offshore and scuttled on October 27, 2001 (Fairplay 2001a).

24) *Orpheus Asia, VLCC.* A very large crude carrier laden with 240,000 tons of crude oil, this hitherto unknown ship suffered engine failure in the Bashi Straits, Southeast Asia. Though Singapore denied the vessel refuge while laden, salvors towed it to an anchorage outside port limits and performed STS operations, after which the Port of Singapore Authority (PSA) permitted entry for repairs. (Same as *Crippled VLCC*, country unknown, casualty dated 12 May 2002) (Oil Spill Report, 2002, 8, ISU, 2005m, 2).

25) *Prestige. Prestige* was denied access to Spanish, French and Portuguese places of refuge, during November 2002. The ship was towed offshore, split in two and sank, spilling most of its cargo of 70,000 tons of heavy oil over the coasts of all three countries. The ship leaked the balance of its cargo during the ensuing two years (Lloyd's Agency, 2005). The facts are covered extensively in the Case Study section of this paper.

26) MSC *Carla.* Mediterranean Shipping Corporation's (MSC) container ship suffered a fire in a container of vegetal coal, in mid-June 2004. The hold was flooded with CO_2. In order to gain the option of a safe place of refuge in nearby Spain, the owners paid a Euro Dollar bond of $1 million. This was to satisfy the royal decree passed 6 February 2004. MSC *Carla* was the first ship to have to pay such a bond to the Spanish following the *Prestige* incident and the IMO Places of Refuge Resolution. Once the crisis was averted, Spain reportedly returned the funds within three days (Lloyd's List, 2004v).

Vessels Granted Places of Refuge: Forty Case Studies

1) *Princess Anne Marie.* A tanker which experienced structural damage west of Australia in the Indian Ocean, was offered a safe STS location off the Dampier Islands in 1975 (CMI, 2002).

2) *Kurdistan.* A British tanker, which developed hull cracks 50 miles northeast of Sydney, Nova Scotia, laden with 29,662 tons of Bunker C fuel, on March 15, 1979. The Canadian Coast Guard advised the tanker to proceed to Sydney, on Cape Breton. However, the ship split in two, the bow sinking and the stern ultimately being salvaged (CMI, 2002).

3) *Tarpenbek.* A coastal tanker carrying 1,785 tons of lubricating oils, the ship was involved in a collision with the *Sir Geraint* 5.2 miles off the English coast on 21 June 1979. Despite vehement local protest, the SOSREP decided to beach the ship in Sandown Bay, Isle of Wight, in order to lighter off persistent oils. Ultimately, the ship was lightered and towed from the beach to Rotterdam for repairs (MAIB, 2005).

4) *Fared Fares.* A livestock carrier which caught fire off of South Australia in 1982. While a request for a place of refuge was being considered, the ship sank with its live cargo (CMI, 2002).

5) *Kowloon Bridge.* Admitted to Bantry Bay, Ireland during 1986 (CMI, 2002).

6) *Trave Ore.* In 1987, Canada refused, then granted access to refuge (CMI, 2002).

7) *Nella Dan.* This vessel ran aground on Australia's Macquarie Island in 1987. While under tow to a place of refuge on the Australian mainland, it sank (CMI, 2002).

8) *Tribulus.* Admitted to Bantry Bay, Ireland during 1990 (CMI, 2002).

9) *Scandinavian Star.* This passenger ship caught fire with 383 passengers and 99 crew aboard between Oslo, Norway and Denmark on April 6th, 1990. On April 7th, Sweden permitted the distressed ship access to Gothenburg port, where the fire was brought under control. 159 persons died in the blaze (CMI, 2002).

10) *Kirki*. A Greek tanker carrying 82,660 tons of light crude oil from the Arabian Gulf to Western Australia. On 20 July, 1991, the ship's hull began to ride down by the bow in severe weather roughly 22 miles from the Australian port of Cervantes. On 21 July, the ship's bow broke off and erupted in fire. The vessel's position was confirmed by a 747 aircraft flying over. The crew were all evacuated by helicopter. The ship was towed to a position roughly 100 miles offshore, where it was lightered by other tankers. After all the cargo was pumped out from a position off the Monte Bello Islands and the Dampier Archipelago, on 19 August, the ship was towed to Singapore for scrapping (CMI, 2002).

11) *Cargo Shift*. A vessel which experienced a dangerous cargo shift during a voyage between Singapore and China was permitted access to Hong Kong for repairs late in 1991, according to that government's statements (CMI, 2002).

12) *Daishowa Maru*. This woodchip carrier ran aground in New South Wales, Australia in 1992. The Australians refused access to Jervis Bay, offering instead Port Kembla. The vessel found a place off refuge in the Great Barrier Reef off Gladstone, Australia before continuing to Japan for repairs (CMI, 2002).

13) *Nagasaki Spirit*. Between the collision and explosion in the Straits of Malacca on 19 September 1992 and return to the ship's owners in Singapore 25 November, Indonesia granted *Nagasaki Spirit* a place of refuge at anchorage where the ship's remaining cargo was transferred to the tanker *Pacific Diamond*.

14) *Darya Tara*. In 1993, this vessel's cargo shifted dangerously while underway. It was welcomed to Brixham, UK, where the cargo was re-stowed. (CMI, 2002).

15) *Mimosa*. In 1995, the *Mimosa* was holed below the waterline 80 miles west of Scotland's Hebrides Islands. She was escorted by two British warships to a place of refuge in Lyme Bay, England (CMI, 2002).

16) *Sea Empress*. In February of 1996, this very large crude oil carrier (VLCC) carrying 130,000 tons of crude oil, ran aground in the approaches to Milford Haven in foul weather, spilling

substantial cargo. For nearly a week, salvors battled to free the ship and shoe-horn it into port. Finally, the ship reached a place of refuge in Milford Haven designated by the UK's SOSREP (CMI, 2002).

17) *Multitank Ascania.* In 1996, an engine-room fire disabled this ship off Scotland. With two escort ships, the *Multitank Ascania* anchored at Dunnet Head, UK to effect repairs and cargo transfer (CMI, 2002).

18) *Ever Decent.* Involved in a collision with the *Norwegian Dream* in the English Channel in 1999, the ship was given access to a place of refuge in Belgium (CMI, 2002).

19) *Norwegian Dream.* After its collision with *Ever Decent* in 1999, the *Norwegian Dream* was allowed to sail to Dover, England, U.K., for repairs (CMI, 2002).

20) *Dole America.* This reefer ship collided with the *Nab Tower* navigational aid in the Solent, England, in 1999. The ship ran aground, was refloated, and towed to Southampton UK, where private dockyard owners refused to attend her (CMI, 2002).

21) *Erika. Enroute* Dunkirk to Sicily with 26,000 tons of heavy fuel oil, *Erika* experienced structural failure in a storm and made for the Loire estuary, France, on 12 December 1999. The French government-run tug *Abeille Flandre* was *enroute* to the tanker when she broke up and sank, an event photographed and published globally. The ship, built 1975, of single-hull and Maltese flag, was abandoned before sinking (Lloyd's List, 2003j).

22) *Blackfriars,* A 992-GT tanker in ballast, ran aground in Saint Bride's Bay, Wales while *enroute* between Dundalk and Milford Haven, during a gale at the end of December, 1999. At first, the Milford Haven Port Control denied the ship harbor access in severe weather. Later, however access to a natural bay anchorage was granted. While at anchor in the storm, the cable parted and the ship ran aground. On the next high tide, the *Blackfriars* was towed off the shore to Pembroke Docks for repair (MAIB, 2005).

23) *Coastal Bay*. In 2000, this ship grounded in Church Bay, Anglesey, western U.K. and was offered access to Liverpool port for repairs, which she achieved under tow (CMI, 2002).

24) *Belofin*. A passenger ship which was enroute to India, to be scrapped, took on a severe list on 21 October, 2001, off of South Africa. Too dangerous to board, the ship sank within seven hours of an aerial inspection by Port Authorities (CMI, 2002).

25) *Sun*. A passenger ship *enroute* to be scrapped around South Africa, the ship took on a severe list and requested permission to enter Algoa Bay on 25 July, 2001. Eighteen hours after an inspection by SAMSA (South African Marine Safety Authority) the ship sank. South Africa claims the ship was offered a place of refuge (CMI, 2002).

26) *Lysfoss*. In 2001, this bulker grounded in the Sound of Mull, UK. It was towed to Salen Bay, where it was inspected and repaired (CMI, 2002).

27) *Kitano*. In 2001, Canada refused, then granted, the ship refuge (CMI, 2002).

28) *Eastern Power*. In 2001 Canada refused, then granted refuge (CMI, 2002).

29) *Ab Bilbao*. This ship suffered an explosion off Margate, in the U.K., in 2001. It was permitted to be towed to a place of refuge in the UK by the SOSREP (CMI, 2002).

30) *Gudermes*. A tanker involved in a collision with the fishing vessel *Saint Jacques II,* in 2001. The Master proceeded to anchorage off of Dover, in the UK for an inspection (CMI, 2002).

31) *Alnar*. A Swedish-registered cargo ship, carrying 168 refugees from civil war in Liberia, during mid-June 2001. Though the governments of Benin, Togo and Ghana turned the ship and its refugees away, Togo did provide some food and water. The *Alnar* was in need of fuel, for which purpose the government of Nigeria permitted them access and agreed to accommodate the refugees (Lloyd's List, 2001f).

32) *Insiko 1907*. An Indonesian tanker, 270 feet long, was carrying 50,000 gallons of petroleum product, when it suffered a severe engine room fires, on March 13, 2002. The crew drifted

with the tanker for 20 days before being rescued by the passenger ship *Norwegian Star*. The U.S. Coast Guard considered scuttling the tanker before it could spill its cargo on ecologically sensitive Johnston Atoll. Ultimately, the ship's dog was rescued after 24 days. The tanker was towed to Honolulu, Hawaii, arriving 2 May 2002.

33) *Willy*. This coastwise German tanker ran aground in Plymouth Sound, UK in 2002. She was later lightered, pressed with air, and towed to Falmouth, UK (CMI, 2002).

34) *Kodima*. In 2002, this ship ran aground in Cornwall, UK, and was permitted to proceed to Falmouth, UK for repairs (CMI, 2002).

35) *Nestor C*. A bulk cargo ship built 1979, flagged to St. Vincent and Grenadines, and blacklisted by European Commission. Ship requested place of refuge roughly 60 miles off Iberian peninsula, on December 2002. The cargo was 30,000 tons of ammonium phosphate. The problem was water ingress through a sea chest. All requests for refuge were flatly refused by Spanish Government. Portuguese officials boarded the ship and agreed to offer it a berth in Sines, south of Lisbon, where *Nestor C* was welcomed and repaired (Tradewinds, 2003b).

36) *Princess Eva*. A Panamanian-flagged 70,000-ton tanker carrying gasoil between Denmark and Texas, the ship lost the Chief and Second Officers to a wave in force 11 weather 130 miles off County Mayo on January 28, 2003. *Princess Eva* then anchored in Killybegs Bay, Ireland. When the Irish Department of Marine officials learned of cracks in the tanker's hull, they welcomed the ship to move to the more sheltered Inver Bay, where *Princess Eva* anchored safely. Between 12 and 21 February, the ship transferred over 54,000 tons of gasoil to the tankers *Princess Pia* and *Bro Jupiter*, enabling it to undergo repairs before returning back to Europe (Lloyd's List, 2003i).

37) *Capella Voyager*. Suezmax tanker laden with 108,000 tons of crude oil enroute from Fujairah, United Arab Emirates, to Whangerei, New Zealand, with a cargo for Caltex. On 16 April 2003, while crossing the bar in heavy seas, the ship touched

bottom twice and ruptured its forepeak tanks. Thousands of tons of water entered the forepeak ballast tanks of the double-hulled tanker. The New Zealand Government welcomed the ship and were accommodating while it underwent repairs. A subsequent investigation found the local pilot and tug company had insufficient technical knowledge of the bar and its effect on large ships (Seatrends, 2003, 1-2).

38) *Bunga Melawis Satu*. A freighter bound from Thailand for mainland China on 4 May 2003, diverted to Hong Kong when 10 of 24 Indian crewmen became ill. Suspected of carrying the severe acute respiratory sickness (SARS) epidemic, the Malaysian-registered ship was permitted to anchor off remote Kau Yi Chau island until inspected and cleared by quarantine officials. Hong Kong officials were following Article 41 of the International Health Regulations in permitting the ship a place of refuge despite concerns of SARS outbreaks (Lloyd's List, 2003m).

39) *Henrietta Kosan*. A 2,323-ton LPG tanker, built in 1982, flagged to the Isle of Man. *Henrietta Kosan* was *enroute* in ballast off Galicia, Spain on April 18, 2004, when problems with the engine's turbo-charger forced the crew to call for help. The Spanish government sent out a tug to assist, which towed the tanker into port (Lloyd's List, 2004u).

40) *Hanjin Pretoria*. A containership *enroute* between China and Long Beach, California, when both main engines abruptly stopped, on 14 December, 2004. The ship's position at the time was roughly 1,000 miles north of Honolulu, Hawaii. Due to a crosshead failure, the crew could not repair the engines. After drifting for six days, a tow was connected, and *Hanjin Pretoria* was towed to Honolulu, where port authorities welcomed the ship and facilitated repairs (Lloyd's List, 2004x).

Table 1, on the following page, summarizes relevant information from these case studies. The perspective and focus is on the role of coastal states worldwide, as in-depth analysis of individual spills is less important to this analysis than a compendium of how different coastal states have reacted to specific, actual instances of disabled vessels seeking places of refuge along their shores. While a vessel is unlikely to make more than two such calls during its career, coastal states may be called upon to respond to places of refuge scenarios dozens of times, depending on their proximity to major shipping routes.

Summary of Places of Refuge Data

During 28 years between 1977 and 2005, 26 ships from a representative sample were denied access to 36 countries that reported their findings to the Comite Maritime International by 2002 (CMI, 2002) or were reported elsewhere. Several ships were rejected by more than one country; the *Castor* by eight, *Khark 5* by five, *Khian Sea* by 11, and *Mobro 4000* by three are examples. The countries which rejected vessels were: the U.K., Ireland, Spain, (for Canaries) France, Portugal (for Azores and Madeira), Gibraltar, Togo, Ghana, Benin, Cape Verde, Malta, Algeria, Tunisia, Cyprus, Greece, Morocco, Brazil, U.S., Belgium, Australia, Singapore, Sri Lanka, South Africa, Namibia, Malaysia, Senegal, Belize, Bahamas, Mexico, Guinea-Bissau, Netherlands Antilles, Haiti, Honduras, Bermuda, and Indonesia. Records for nations like Russia (former U.S.S.R.), Japan, China, and India are not available.

During 30 years between 1975 and 2005, 40 ships were provided with places of refuge, or the option of taking places of refuge without undue financial bond, in 17 countries, according to those country's own statistics provided to the Comite Maritime International in 2002 (CMI, 2002) (barring Japan, China, Russia/U.S.S.R., and India).

The countries that granted places of refuge were Australia, the UK, Canada, Ireland, Sweden, Hong Kong, Belgium, Spain, France, South Africa, Nigeria, U.S., Portugal, New Zealand, Yugoslavia, Indonesia, and Haiti. Although this is not an exhaustive study, it represents a fairly comprehensive search of available contemporary literature on places of refuge, a topic of considerable interest and scholarship in light of the *Erika, Castor* and *Prestige* incidents. More importantly, according to the methodology, as more data become known, new variables may be reliably plugged in to the equation to provide results such as swings in trends over time. The statistically significant difference between 26 ships denied access versus 40 that were granted places of refuge suggests that coastal states are more receptive than much of the lobby-oriented literature would have one believe.

Furthermore, of all the countries, which either granted or denied places of refuge, 11 out of the 35 that rejected vessels later accepted others. This represents roughly one third, or 35 percent of 'rejecting' countries also being 'accepting' countries under different circumstances. Of the 17 countries, which have accepted ships in distress, 11 have also rejected them. This indicates that roughly two thirds, or 65 percent of those countries which accepted ships, were also experienced at rejecting them under different circumstances. This represents a higher percentage than those countries that rejected, but never accepted, vessels in distress.

One tentative conclusion is that countries are 30 percent, or one third, more likely to reject ships than accept them, and that countries, which have rejected some ships are less likely to accept others in the future. Spain's example would appear to bear this out, having rejected eight ships and only accepted one from this survey. The U.K., on the other hand, has an impressive record of accepting the overwhelming number of casualties reported; the U.K. have accepted 15 casualties in this time-frame and only rejected three. While it would appear that some countries exhibit almost predictable patterns of behavior, and Morocco, Brazil and Sri Lanka are all 'rejecters,' the majority of countries that have rejected ships have accepted roughly the same number of ships, with a differential of only one to three ships, out of an average of four places of refuge incidents. The results, while inconclusive, provide at least one snapshot of activity over 30 years.

TABLE 1:

COUNTRIES THAT DENIED OR GRANTED PLACES OF REFUGE 1975-2005

Denied Refuge (How Often)
(How Often)

1. U.K. (3)
2. Spain (incl. Canaries) (7)
3. Portugal (incl. Madeira, Azores) (4)
4. Ireland (1)
5. Belgium (1)
6. Haiti (1)
7. South Africa (3)
8. Indonesia (1)
9. Australia (2)
10. France (3)
11. U.S. (1)
12. Mexico (1)
13. Belize (1)
14. Bahamas (1)
15. Brazil (2)
16. Morocco (2)
17. Togo (1)
18. Cyprus (1)
19. Gibraltar (1)
20. Cape Verde (1)
21. Namibia (1)
22. Malaysia (1)
23. Sri Lanka (2)
24. Guinea-Bissau (1)
25. Benin (1)
26. Ghana (1)
27. Senegal (2)
28. Tunisia (1)

Granted Refuge

1. U.K. (15)
2. Spain (1)
3. Portugal (1)
4. Ireland (3)
5. Belgium (1)
6. Haiti (1)
7. South Africa (1)
8. Indonesia (1)
9. Australia (5)
10. France (1)
11. U.S. (2)
12. Hong Kong (2)
13. Canada (4)
14. Yugoslavia (1)
15. New Zealand (1)
16. Nigeria (1)
17. Sweden (1)

Countries (Totals: Deny/Grant):

1. U.K. (18: 3/15)
2. Spain (8: 7/1)
3. Portugal (5: 4/1)
4. Ireland (4: 1/3)
5. Belgium (2: 1/1)
6. Haiti (2: 1/1)
7. South Africa (4: 3/1)

29. Malta (1)
30. Netherlands Antilles (1)
31. Singapore (1)
32. Algeria (1)
33. Dominican Republic (1)
34. Bermuda (1)
35. Honduras (1)
36. Greece (1)

8. Indonesia (2: 1/1)
9. Australia (7: 2/5)
10. France (4: 3/1)
11. U.S. (3: 1/2)
Top 11 Totals: 27 Deny/32 Grant
Totals: 42 countries, 65 casualties
Top 11: 59 of 66 casualties, or c90%

Eight Countries That Have Composed/Published Places of Refuge Lists, 2003-2005:

Indonesia, Denmark, Germany, Spain, U.K., Norway, New Zealand, and Singapore.

Sources: CMI, 2002, Hayward, 2002, Greenpeace, 2004, News of Odd, 2004, Penelope, 2002, Fairplay, 2001a, Semco,1997, Lloyd's Agency, 2005, Lloyd's Ship Manager, 2000, ISU, 2005, MAIB, 2005, Tradewinds, 2003b, Seatrends, 2003, Lloyd's List International, 2001f, 2001g, 2003i, 2003j, 2003m, 2004u, 2004x, author's own research and tabulation.

Interestingly, the 11 most active countries have handled 59 of the 66 casualties listed, or 90 percent, suggesting that a dozen or so strategically places coastal states actually are highly determinative of places of refuge outcomes. It seems that the ISU and IMO should focus on these core states, namely the U.K., Spain, Portugal, Ireland, Belgium, Indonesia, South Africa, Australia and France, as this cabal seem to have almost cornered the market on refuge incidents. Of the eight states that have published lists, only U.K. and Spain are on the core list. Denmark, Norway, New Zealand, and tentatively Singapore and Indonesia, are more peripheral to the core study.

CHAPTER 5

PARIAH SHIP: MT *CASTOR*, 2000-2001

Facts of the *Castor* Voyage

The lengthy and titillating saga of the Motor Tanker (MT) *Castor* illustrates just how harmful it has turned out for salvors to allow the P&I Club and Owners to shirk and avoid SCOPIC, placing most of the costs on Hull Underwriters (Lloyd's Agency, 2005a). The saga of the *Castor* is a memorable one, analogous to the voyages of the barges *Khian Sea* and *Mobro 4000, l*aden with U.S. ash and trash, respectively. The barges were rebuffed by a dozen states and countries worldwide during the 1980s (Hayward, 2002).

During severe weather between December 26th and 31st, 2000, the motor tanker *Castor* (Cypriot-flagged, Greek owned, 18,565 gross tons, built 1977, and single-hull) developed a crack as long as 66 feet long, by one millimeter wide across its deck and freeboard, by way of the number four cargo tank. It was carrying a cargo of 29,500 metric tons of unleaded gasoline from the Black Sea port of Constanza, Romania, to Lagos, Nigeria. Immediately, the owners ordered it to the nearest port, which was Nador, Mediterranean Morocco, mere hours away, for inspection and possible repairs. There was no cargo egress, and the weather was still boisterous (Lloyd's List, 2005, 13-14).

The owners, Athenian Sea Carriers, and the classification society, the American Bureau of Shipping, assigned three inspectors to meet the vessel in Morocco. A tug was deployed which met the *Castor*. The crew were unharmed, and the ship's machinery was operational, about 18 miles off the coast. On January 4th, 2001, the Moroccan Coast Guard ordered the vessel to proceed to 40 miles from the coast. They also denied it access to the port of Nador, or any other Moroccan port or refuge. This treatment of the *Castor* as a leper-ship continued for one and a half months, with the port state controls of Spain, Gibraltar, Morocco,

99

Algeria, Tunisia, Greece, Cyprus, and Malta denying the vessel a place of refuge in which to effect lightering operations.

Lightering refers to a cargo transfer operation, called STS, for ship-to-ship transfer, involves tankers coming alongside one another without any fixed structures, and connecting cargo hoses to pump cargo from one ship to the other. It can be a complicated, dangerous operation, and is best done in the shelter of land, or in windless, calm conditions at anchor. Steel ships carrying and exuding thousands of tons of gasoline, when forced to gently collide and rub alongside one another in open seas can generate sparks. In such a highly flammable and volatile environment, any metal-on-metal contact is highly dangerous.

In this case, the immediate danger was not so much of pollution, since most agree that non-leaded gasoline in turbulent seas and hot weather would evaporate more quickly than most other forms of petroleum. The greatest dangers to the *Castor* were explosion resulting from grating of steel plates aboard the vessel. This was mitigated by crew continuously pouring water over the serrated steel. Hull collapse followed by sinking also presented a distinct danger to the ship's crew and salvage crew.

From Nador, *Castor* proceeded under escort of tugs, and, later of two lightering tankers under charter by owners. First the convoy approached the adjacent coast of Spain and Gibraltar. Spain would prove the coastal state to most stringently deny *Castor* refuge, perhaps setting a precedent for other countries.

There was a misunderstanding of the definition of port of refuge. The Spanish claimed it meant an along-side berth in an active commercial port. The salvors and owner say they only needed a sheltered, uninhabited, anchor-able bay in which to carry out a STS transfer. Spain refused the ship access to its shore, its naval and merchant equipment, and its port facilities for STS operations, lightering, anchoring, or discharge. They even refused a lightering ship, the 6,800-ton *Giovanna*, which had taken several thousand tons of gasoline from the *Castor,* access to its ports to discharge conventionally, though the vessel was fully classed and self-propelled (Lloyd's List, 2005, 6).

This is a typical entry in the Lloyd's Casualty Reports for *Castor*, dated contemporaneously and circulated utilizing the Lloyd's network in print and Internet. Even the most hardened readers can sense the salvor's and writer's frustration and anger:

> The crew of motor tanker *Castor* abandoned ship Friday (Jan. 5, 2001), after officials in Morocco, Gibraltar and Spain ruled the vessel was too dangerous to allow ashore. *Castor* was being towed away from Spain's southeastern shore by the tug *Nikolay Chiker*. On the basis that no port of refuge was available, the master of the vessel, supported by the managers, had no choice but to abandon the vessel. Spanish authorities said the crack across the main deck of *Castor* ran the width of the vessel and other cracks were appearing. They ordered the tanker to move at least 30 miles (48 km) off Spain's coast and recommended evacuation of the Polish crew. The Spanish meteorological office forecast strong winds and heavy seas in the area. Authorities in the southern Andalusia said they were monitoring the situation (Lloyd's Agency, 2005, 12-13).

Figure 5, following page, provides a general idea of the geography involved as *Castor* retraced its way eastwards from the mouth to the depths of the Mediterranean past Morocco, Spain, Gibraltar, Algeria, Tunisia, Cyprus, Malta, and Greece on its inexorable way back to Piraeus.

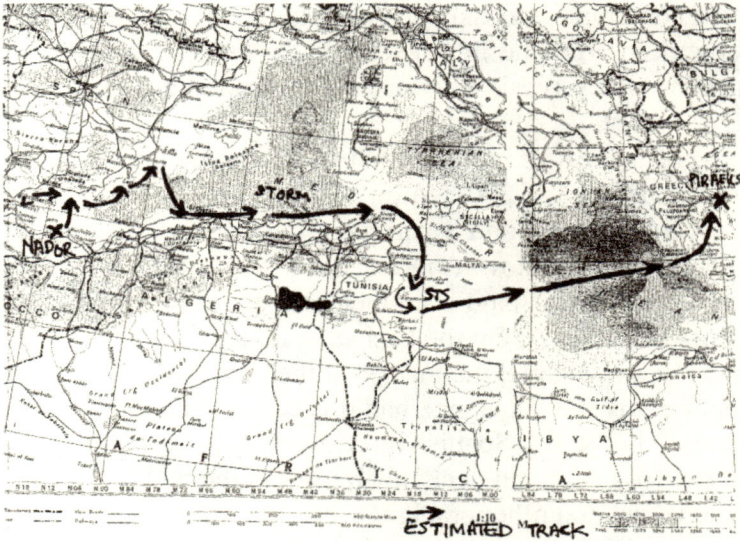

FIGURE 5:
MAP SHOWING ROUTE OF MT *CASTOR*, 2000-2001
Source: Bartholomew, (1974), and Author's input tracing
Castor's course.

The Spanish, having forced the evacuation of all but essential or salvage crew and master, considered its obligation to the casualty as having been met, and ignored all appeals by affected parties, international organizations; IMO, ABS, and ISMA, (the
International Ship Manager's Association). Spain further alleged that the vessel was substandard, an allegation countered with surprising unanimity by Cyprus, ABS, the vessel owners and insurers. In fact, later investigation did show signs of 'hyper-accelerated rust' on the starboard ballast tanks, which had lost significant protective coatings. The owners and ABS counter-argued that the six weeks' of rough handling during denial of a place of refuge oxygenated the cargo tanks and mixed salt water and gasoline, both highly corrosive, with steel superstructure, accelerating the corrosion.

On the night of January 19th, as the convoy rode out bad weather, a mystery ship actually steamed right over the 750 meter wire cable connecting *Castor* to the attached tug, *Nikolay Chiker*. For the 50 crew on the *Chiker* and ten or so on *Castor*, it was a very tense experience, and the other vessel refused to respond to signals or radio. Fortunately the ship cleared the slacked cable. It continued on, unrecognized (Lloyd's Agency, 2005 7). The salvage operation meanwhile was costing the owners roughly US$1 million a week. The following press release reads like a requiem to the *Castor*'s travails:

> Jan. 18: Cyprus, as country of registry for motor tanker *Castor*, has begun making contingency plans for a possible scuttling of the damaged tanker with her cargo on board. The Cypriot government believes that, after more than two weeks of failing to gain shelter off the coast of Spain, it is becoming increasingly likely that efforts to salvage the vessel will ultimately have to be abandoned. The flag state's pessimism came to light as two further international shipping bodies joined

the chorus of complaint aimed at Spain and other coastal states which have turned their back on the vessel's plight. By yesterday, the ISMA and ISU had both condemned the attitude of countries refusing to allow the stricken tanker to gain refuge closer to their coasts. Cyprus alone has said it would be prepared to harbor the *Castor* under agreed conditions (Lloyd's Agency, 2005, 6).

The Maltese also reneged on their offer of refuge. In Cyprus, the decision went as far as a special joint session of the Cabinet. Still no refuge offered. By February 1st,

> The damaged and shunned motor tanker *Castor* has not been given permission to berth in Malta. The Transport Ministry yesterday strongly denied reports that the tanker was being allowed to berth anywhere near the Maltese coast. The Malta Maritime Authority is monitoring the situation and checking what international obligations it has towards this vessel, the ministry said. The vessel has so far been refused by Morocco, Gibraltar, Spain, Algeria, and Greece (Lloyd's Agency, 2001, 6).

Meanwhile, the *Castor* proceeded at a slow speed, and beset by severe weather, in an easterly direction, the salvors all the while lobbying for a government or port state authority to permit them access to facilities to repair and discharge their cargo. On February 16th, bereft of her cargo and finally suitable for the operating table, Castor was towed into Piraeus Harbor, Greece. Nearly two months had passed since she passed Athens on the way from the Black Sea (Lloyd's Agency, 2002, 5). The *Castor* had finally made a port, not during the storm, but after the six long storm-beaten weeks, from western to eastern Mediterranean. *Castor* got by, but with very little help from her friends. Even during the casualty, it was recognized by the participants that something would need to be done about places of refuge:

> Spain, at the heart of the controversy over the future of *Castor*, is keen to keep the ports of refuge issue alive within the IMO, but cautioned that such ports cannot be imposed on governments. While salvor Tsavliris yesterday continued efforts to inert the entire vessel and render her gasoline cargo safe, Esteban Pach, Spain's permanent representative at the IMO, stressed the need for continued debate over ports of refuge. Mr. Pach said: 'We want to examine whether the experiences of the *Castor* incident can be used as the basis for a document, to be submitted to the next IMO Marine Safety Committee meeting, on how ports of refuge should be organized. We have to see how we handle the experience of *Castor*. Once we can analyze it in its entirety, could provide a positive contribution to the debate.' But, reflecting the position of the govern-ments that have to date refused shelter to the disabled vessel, he added: 'Ports of refuge cannot be imposed on governments or states' (Lloyd's Agency, 2005, 6).

What differentiates this case from that of *Prestige*, *Exxon Valdez,* or *Braer* is that the vessel was manned pretty much continuously, and in imminent danger of breaking up and sinking, until when it was finally able to return to Piraeus, Greece, where its owners are based, for repairs. That the ship survived force 12 storms (hurricane force) for days in end January shows how strong the *Castor* actually was. Several countries, including Cyprus, Greece, and Tunisia, made half-hearted offers to help, while the Spanish, by not permitting the 6,800 DWT lighter-ship *Giovanna* access to its shore, actually obstructed operations. The closest the salvors received to an act of kindness was Tunisia permitting the ship to lighter the balance cargo of 23,000 tons 100 miles or so off of that country's huge natural bays. Because they provided no refuge until after the ship was clean of cargo, Greece deserves little credit. One by one, each potentially helpful coastal state prevaricated and vacillated. In the end, salvors had to empty the ship on their own.

Legal Synopsis of *Castor* Salvage Claim

The *Castor* case was unlike the later *Prestige* incident in that the vessel owners and P&I Club opted out of the SCOPIC clause. They were rewarded heartily for doing so.
On appeal the salvors, on the other hand, lost all of the funds beyond labor and out-of-pocket expenses. Their reward was reduced by a staggering US$2.4 million. The absence of invocation of the SCOPIC clause of the Lloyd's Open Form relegated the salvors to an Article 13 or 14 claim under the 1989 International Salvage Convention. In August of 2003, the appointed appeal arbitrator Nigel Teare, Q.C. used these clauses to deprive the salvor of one third (US$2.4 million) of the original US$8 million award (Lloyd's Agency 2005, 1). As a result of this finding, Tsavliris, a major player in the global salvage market and an active member of the ISU, assessed their status in the industry thus:

> Tsavliris' managing director Xenophon Constantinides acknowledged the company was 'shocked.' He said "We thought it was a question of how much, not whether there would be any compensation at all. It is very discouraging, and we will now review the company's position in the market." Lawyer Richard Gunn said that as the Article 14 award is now less than the Article 13 award, this will be met wholly by hull underwriters… the club "will have got a windfall" (Lowry, 2002, 3).
> The proceeding will be the most important legal test of article 14, which is ultimately meant to help protect the environment, since the *Nagasaki*

Spirit case, which decided what is meant by 'fair rate' for salvor's expenses... "The failure to earn an uplift in the case with the *Castor*'s characteristics will have a 'serious impact' on the salvage industry and the environment in the future." Tsavliris is claiming the chopping of its Article 14 award has left it with remuneration that barely covers is expenses, causing wide concern among other salvors as well as the ISU (Lloyd's Agency, 2005, 1-2).

At the conclusion of the case, Lloyd's Casualty Desk surmised that "the application of Article 14 of the Salvage Convention has once again proved to be the subject of debate when Tsavliris' *Castor* award was knocked down on appeal. The salvage company has applied to the English High Court for leave to appeal against the decision after $2.4m awarded in special compensation under Article 14 was overturned" (Lloyd's List, 2002h). There has been no indication since that Tsavliris won any appeal.

Castor Compared with Barges *Khian Sea* and *Mobro 4000*

Perhaps surprisingly, the *Castor* was not the only ship deprived of a place of refuge for weeks – or even years. Author Hayward (2002) tracks the dubious career of another pariah, the *Khian Sea*. For two years, between September, 1986 and November 1988, "the *Khian Sea* sailed around the world, trying to find a country – any country – that would accept [its cargo of ash] for disposal. The *Khian Sea* originally had a contract with the Bahamas to accept the ash, but, *enroute*, the Bahamian government changed it mind and reneged. The *Khian Sea* tried several other Caribbean and Central American nations without success" (Hayward, 2002, 1-3).

The *Khian Sea* voyaged to Guinea-Bissau, Senegal, and Cape Verde, trying to pay to unload the industrial ash. But by then the word of its notoriety had leaked out, and there were no takers. Like the *Castor*, the barge made its way forlornly eastwards: Sri Lanka, Indonesia, Borneo, and the Philippines all rejected her. After transiting Asia, *Khian Sea* was towed back to the United States, where they reportedly "even tried the Cherokee Nation in Oklahoma" as a venue for their unwanted cargo (Greenpeace, 2005).

> During its *Flying Dutchman* odyssey around the world, the ship was turned away from some ports at gunpoint, the crew mutinied, and two executives of the shipping company went to prison for ordering the crew to dump the ash over the side in the middle of the ocean. The ship was sold once and renamed twice, apparently hoping it could slip its unwanted cargo by a harbormaster under a different name. Finally Pennsylvania agreed to take back its trash and bury it in a local landfill, near where it came from in the first place (Hayward, 2002, 1-3).

The *Khian Sea* episode was not unique. It could be compared to the contemporary voyage of the *Mobro 4000* garbage barge. One obvious distinction against the *Castor* episode is that the *Mobro 4000* and *Khian Sea* were not apparently in danger of sinking, nor were the lives of the men put at immediate risk by the refusal of a place of refuge, though, if mutiny is any indication, they crew were taxed. Put in perspective,

> What the *Khian Sea* episode teaches is that the NIMBY ("Not-In-My-Back-Yard") phenomenon has gone worldwide, aided, of course, by some rabble-rousing from Greenpeace, which made the *Khian Sea* a *cause-celebre*. One reason

this absurd episode got carried to such length is that
a similar episode on a smaller scale once galvanized
the recycling movement. In the late 1980s TV news
viewers were treated to nightly images of the
infamous *Mobro* garbage barge trawling up and
down the Atlantic seaboard looking for a place to
unload its trash heap, which originated in New York
(Hayward, 2002, 2).

The barge *Mobro 4000* and its escort, the tug *Break of Day*
left New York with 3,200 tons of trash on March 22, 1987. During
the next six months, the duo traveled 6,000 miles along the U.S.
eastern seaboard, the Gulf of Mexico, and Yucatan, Mexico. Its
cargo was rejected by several states in the U.S., then Mexico,
Belize, and the Bahamas. In October, 1987, the trash was
converted to 430 tons of ash and buried in Islip, NY. Like the
Khian Sea, the *Mobro 4000* returned to its roost (News of the Odd,
2004). These narratives serve to grasp the reader's attention by the
sheer implausibility and also to illustrate the longevity of some
instances of denial of a place of refuge. Several cases went on for
months, and some for years; the damaged cargo ship *Smirdan*
loitered off Singapore for three years in 1997, before being sold at
one percent of its value. The *Protokletas* waited nine months off a
Brazilian port in 1992 awaiting refuge before being scuttled with
its cargo, and the tanker *Ventura* sank off Sri Lanka after waiting
three months for refuge in 1999. The aim of exposing these case
studies is to show that they occurred, and to use them to illustrate
the downside of denial of refuge.

CHAPTER 6

CASTOFF: MT *PRESTIGE*, 2002-2004

Facts of the *Prestige* Voyage and Oil Spill

The lengthy saga of the motor tanker *Prestige* illustrates just how beneficial SCOPIC can be to salvors who secure its coverage for their services. This is particularly true when, as with the *Castor*, governments deny distressed vessels access to the nearest place of refuge. The facts of the *Prestige* bear at least summarizing here, as they offer extraordinary parallels with the facts of the *Castor* and other cases in all but the dire outcome. As in that earlier incident, a worst-case-scenario began unfolding as a result of government refusal to allow a tanker access to a place of refuge in which to transship cargo. However, while the *Castor* managed to hold itself together through several onslaughts of severe weather, the *Prestige*, out in the North Atlantic, was not able to do so. If the Spanish authorities hoped that the *Prestige* incident would end like the *Castor* calamity the year before, they were grossly mistaken. Whether or not the Spanish government is to blame for the environmental disaster; the worst in its history, remains to be seen. Three years later, the political, economic and environmental assessment is still ongoing.

After four months of ship-to-ship operations in St. Petersburg, Russia, following a voyage from a repair yard in China, *Prestige* departed on October 30th 2002 partly laden with a cargo of heavy fuel oil (only about 2,000 tons). The ship arrived in Ventspils, Latvia, in the Baltic, by the first of November. There it took on the balance of a cargo totaling, 77,000 metric tons. The charterers were a joint Russian/Swiss trading house named Crown Resources. On the fifth of November *Prestige* cleared Latvia, arriving off of Kerteminde, Denmark the same day in order to bunker. On the seventh of November, the ship cleared the Baltic Sea, and on the tenth passed Dover, U.K.. *Prestige* was bound for Singapore via another bunker stop off Gibraltar.

Prestige was a Bahamas-flagged, 1976-built, single-hulled, American Bureau of Shipping-classed motor tanker with a total deadweight cargo capacity of 81,564 metric tons; so she sailed with 4,500 tons below cargo capacity, probably to account for the severe winter north Atlantic weather and its effect on the Plimsoll load-line. (Lloyd's Agency, 2005, 28). During the passage across the notorious Bay of Biscay, the vessel experienced very severe weather, of force ten magnitude (the maximum is force twelve). The same storm knocked containers and telephone poles from ships in the vicinity as it rounded the chokepoint of Cape Finisterre, Galicia, northwest Spain.

On November 13, 2002 *Prestige* experienced a sudden hull rupture, possibly as a result of an allision (contact between ship and another object) or structural failure, and immediately began to list to starboard. One of her ballast tanks connected to the outer hull had ruptured. The ship was only 26.5 nautical miles off the Spanish coast, or just over two hours away at 12 knots. The crew mustered at their stations, and the Master transmitted a Mayday. Within four hours, the tug *Ria De Vigo* was on-site to assist the vessel. *Prestige* soon developed a list of between 25 and 35 degrees, which the crew tried to correct by pumping liquids to the high, or non-listing port side, to no avail. On 14 November, 24 crewmembers were evacuated. Three officers, including the master, Apostolos Mangouras, then aged 68, remained on board. Early in the casualty, on the night of the 13th, the vessel's owners, Universe Marine of Piraeus, Greece, signed not only LOF 2000 but also SCOPIC 2000. Tugs began towing the *Prestige* away from the Spanish coast. By November 15, Spanish navy vessels were escorting the tanker that was leaking a slick of crude oil from ruptured tanks number three (tanks on tankers are numbered from fore to aft and are normally three across on a ship of *Prestige*'s size). The engines had been shut down, restarted, shut down again, all on command from Spanish officials including their engineer, the master claimed (Lloyd's Agency, 2005, 34-35).

Regarding causes, the flag-state, the Bahamas Maritime Authority, relates:

When the incident occurred, the [BMA] was
notified that a piece of the shell planting in way of
the number three starboard ballast [not cargo] tank
had fallen away. As a result, the ship took a sudden
list, and some cargo was discharged onto the deck.
No cargo tanks were breached. This situation
remained unchanged for a further 36 hours, during
which time the vessel was ordered further out to sea
and was towed 244 kilometers (152 miles) away
from the coast (BMA, 2003, 1).

A tug-of-war ensued, during which the *Prestige* variously
drifted, or was towed, to as few as thee miles to as many as 100
miles from the Spanish coast. By November 15th, it was leaking a
20-mile long slick of fuel oil. On at least two occasions at the
outset, it seemed the ship would wash ashore imminently. Given
that the *Urquiola* spilled 101,000 tons in nearby La Coruna in
1976, followed by the *Aegean Sea* wrecking there with 80,000 tons
in 1992, the Spanish had cause to be concerned. The Spanish
government consistently ordered the *Prestige* to be towed beyond a
120-mile line; an arbitrary line, not based on either the continental
shelf or any 200-mile Exclusive Economic Zone (EEZ). During the
operation, the weather remained characteristic of the Bay of Biscay
in the winter: atrocious. It varied between Beaufort Force 5 and
11. The steep, choppy seas and heavy winds complicated salvage
efforts, and exacerbated the strain on the vessel's structure. Figure
6, following page, details *Prestige*'s final voyage.

On November 15th, the Spanish government arrested the
vessel's Greek master. On November 17th, the Spanish
government, which along with the governments of France and
Portugal had denied access to their places of refuge, ordered the
salvors on the *Prestige* to stop the vessel roughly 100 miles from
the Spanish coast. This entailed *Prestige* shutting down her power
plant permanently.

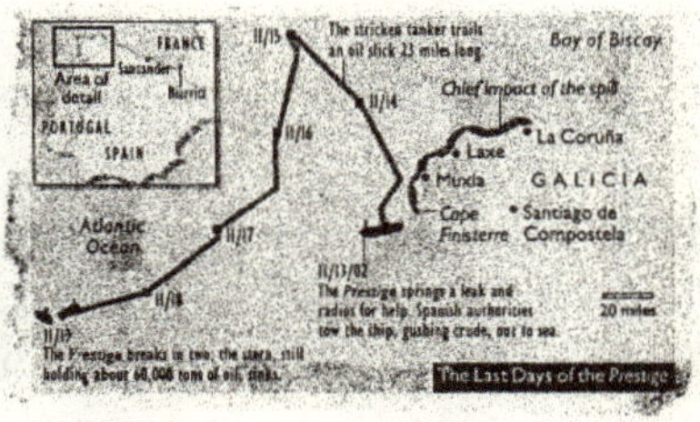

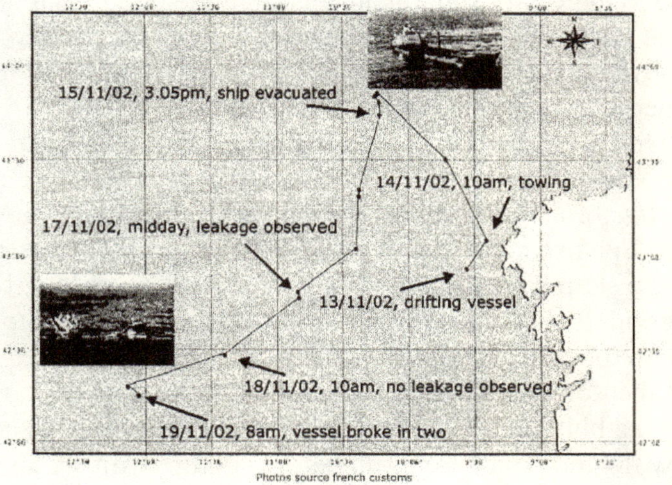

FIGURE 6:
TWO MAPS SHOWING SINKING OF MT. *PRESTIGE*, 2002
Source: Tayler, (2005), and CEDRE, (2005), www.le-cedre.fr/uk/spill/prestige.html

Prestige was thus no longer able to assist salvors or herself in following Madrid's instructions on heading to sea.

The convoy remained off the Spanish coast, in international waters, awaiting instruction. They were badly treated by severe weather. Spanish officials meanwhile assured the fishing and tourism-dependent communities in Galicia and La Coruna, probably sincerely, that they had the resources and ability to protect and rehabilitate any environmental damage. They were resigned to the vessel sinking, and assured the public that the crude oil would not escape from the vessel, should it sink in deep water. Up to November 17, the *Prestige* is estimated to have lost roughly 5,000 metric tons of crude oil into the ocean.

On November 19th, while being towed in convoy of four tugs in a southerly direction in an attempt to escape severe gales, the *Prestige* broke in two. Her position at the time was roughly 140 miles the Spanish coast, due west of Vigo. Shortly after breaking in two, the stern section sank, followed several hours later by the bow section. It was untenable for tugs to remain attached to it. Television footage captured, and relayed, images of a large gash at least 33 feet long in the vessel's starboard side, at which point some of the hull had staved in. The ship bent inward and snapped. The bow floated pointed-end-up before sinking with a sigh. This was filmed from a helicopter. Figure 7, following page, depicts two of the images showing Prestige as it was breaking up.

Due to crew reports of a loud crack or 'explosion-like' noise immediately preceding the vessel taking on a list, speculation arose as to whether a cargo of logs lost overboard the day of the incident (12 November), or a cluster of containers lost the previous week, may have caused an allission. No evidence of this has surfaced, despite numerous dives on the hull since. Spanish authorities, as with *Castor*, hinted at structural weaknesses, due, they said, to many STS transfers carried out over four months in St. Petersburg. They flung accusations of criminal negligence at the master.

The casualty, as seen through the eyes of the salvor's lobby ISU, reads thus:

The salvor recognized the realities of the situation from the first. This fully-laden tanker had suffered structural damage and was leaking cargo. While a tug had reached her, and had just managed to prevent her grounding, the fate of the *Prestige* and the cargo remained in the balance. The choice before the authorities was unpalatable, to say the least. The Salvage Master requested a safe haven and his request was refused. The potential price of refusal was the loss of both ship and cargo. In this extreme case the price was paid in full. The weakened hull of the *Prestige* could not withstand the violence of the Winter Atlantic (ISU, 2005, 2).

FIGURE 7:
PHOTOGRAPHS OF MT *PRESTIGE* SINKING, 2002
Sources: Deutsche World (2005), and CNN (2005)

The classification society (ABS), the International Association of Classification Societies, the Bahamas Maritime Authority, and the vessel owners (Mare Shipping), vigorously defended the vessel; the charterers generally lay low. Rows between Spanish and British governments over the vessel's intent to call in at Gibraltar also created political ruckus. Portugal's decision to elevate the alert status of their Navy raised eyebrows, as did top-level meetings between the leaders of France and Spain. These all created a flurry of activity afloat and ashore, closely covered by the press. Like the *Erika*, *Prestige*'s loss turned out to be a very photogenic one. The bow section succumbed to the elements and sank, roughly five miles from where the stern had gone down.

When the hulls sank there were roughly 55,000 metric tons of fuel oil on board. The depth was 11,550 feet, or roughly three miles. At the time of the sinking, it was estimated that 295 miles of Galician coastline had been harmed, and that the initial damage would cost at least US$41 million to mitigate, of which the shipowner's insurer (London Club) would pay US$25 million, the balance to be covered by the International Oil Pollution Fund (which made Euro $178 million available) (Lloyd's Agency, 2005, 29). In fact, the spill would end up affecting roughly 1,900 kilometers of coast and may cost close to US$7 billion, or roughly $5 billion Euro. It took one week, from the 13th to 19th of November, for the *Prestige* to pack it in. It would take another two years to stop oil from leaking from the hulls. Because crude oil floats, the hulls leaked prodigiously.

The *Prestige*'s Master "claimed that his ship had collided with a floating object and sprung a leak. Rather than offer a port of refuge, Spanish authorities evacuated most of the crew by helicopter and sent tugboats to tow the derelict craft out to sea, apparently planning to abandon it in Portuguese waters. Cape Finisterre, north of the Spanish and Portuguese frontier, translates as 'End of the World' in Galician - a cliff-bound finger of cape jutting into the thrashing Atlantic. Known for its violent seas since ancient times, the 'Coast of Death' has taken many mariners' lives" (Tayler, 2004, 80-81).

Political Consequences of *Prestige* Oil Spill

Despite the initial assurances of the Spanish government, who were perhaps trying to atone for their having unwittingly created a scatter effect of the oil, thick oil continued to seep upwards from numerous leaks in both sections of *Prestige*'s hull and wash ashore. On the surface, the oil would aggregated with salty, cold surf and increase up to four times in volume and weight. The pollution severely coated coastal regions, dampening the economies in Portugal, France, and, most markedly, Spain, where the *Prestige* is considered the worst environmental disaster in that country's long history.

The political fallout of the spill continues. Spain filed a US$5 billion lawsuit against the ABS, alleging negligent certification. The case was removed from Texas to New York in May of 2004 (Lloyd's Agency, 2005, 7). Conversely, certain Spanish, government ministers, including the minister of merchant marine most responsible for rebuffing the *Castor*, came under criminal suit by plaintiffs in Galicia, who blamed them for negligence and mismanagement of the casualty, and for increasing the damage inflicted on their coast (Lloyd's Agency, 2005, 16).

Damage assessment by the World Wildlife Fund (WWF) places total cleanup cost as upwards of US$6 billion over ten years, possibly surpassing the awards and penalties assessed against Exxon in the *Exxon Valdez* incident over a decade earlier. The *Prestige* looks to be the single-most costly oil-tanker spill in history. It may well take a generation from the ship's demise to calculate the final costs. The wreck gave credence to a French word describing paranoia of oil spills – "*psychose*" (Tayler, 2004, 85).

In France the response was a marked contrast to that adopted by Spain; "On December 22, 2002, a squall carried the *mare noire* ashore. In anticipation, the government had activated its environmental emergency plans: Pomar on December 3, when the oil was still 150 miles away; and Polmar Terre on December 7, when patches of oil were spotted some 12 miles off the coast. Beaches were closed, reconnaissance planes and helicopters patrolled the skies, searching for slicks at sea; nets were stretched a mile out from sensitive coastal areas; fishing and oyster–gathering were suspended; and a total of 955 soldiers, firemen, fishermen, and volunteers mobilized to deal with the mess. The French environmental watchdog association *Cedre* counts 41,000 tons of fuel collected and 5,00 tons evaporated, which leaves 17,000 tons lurking in the sea at large, awaiting propitious winds to strike the coast (Tayler, 2004, 80-85).

The political fur continues to fly. In contrast to the *Castor*, which had a much happier ending for the owners and the insurers, the salvors of the *Prestige* can at least anticipate remuneration for their part in mitigating environmental disaster, thanks to the fact that they contracted under SCOPIC, the Special Compensation Clause. This protects salvors for having had to follow the orders of the Spanish government, serve in a hostile environment, and ultimately lose the vessel unnecessarily. Ironically, salvors may be paid more, proportionately, more for losing the *Prestige* than Tsavliris received for saving the *Castor*.

Interestingly, the collateral which insurers were to put up under SCOPIC is US$3 million – roughly the same amount used to bond and bail *Prestige*'s Master. In their description of Places of Refuge, the IMO stresses the element of 'balancing of interests of the affected ship with those of the environment" (IMO, 2005, 1).

The Spanish govern-ment simultaneously offered to pay the same amount (US$3 million) for the cleanup of 65,000 metric tons or so of fuel oil on their coast as they were demanding for the release of a 68-year-old sea captain. Balancing of interests at work.

The latest updates from Lloyd's Casualty Desk, U.K., provide the following:

> Two years after Spain's worst environmental disaster, the country is still reeling from the costs to the environment caused by tens of thousands of tons of leaked oil. The financial cost has been no less great after an ambitious operation to pump out oil from the wreck and the clean-up after a spillage that polluted hundreds of beaches halfway up the western French coastline. A Government spokeswoman, says the bill has topped an estimated one billion Euros to date, with more than 100 million Euros placed into pumping out nearly 14,000 tons of fuel from the wreck. The disaster also crippled the fishing industry in largely rural Galicia, severely affecting tourism, a mainstay for the local economy (Lloyd's Agency, 2005, 1).

As would be expected, one of Spain's most vocal critics is the ISU, whose people were literally turned away at Spain's doorstep and forced take a battering at sea in an already-pulverized tanker:

> Predictably, the spill was followed by a vigorous search for scapegoats. This had all the atmosphere of a 17th Century witch-hunt. Many controversial questions still surround the loss of the *Prestige*, but few would dispute that the safe haven issue was critical to the outcome. In rather crude terms, the decision to order the tanker out was a €5 billion gamble that failed. There was only one way to save *Prestige*, and that was to accept limited pollution and grant a place of refuge. Many safe

havens were available in the area; some just a few
hours away (ISU, 2004, 6).

Environmental Consequences of *Prestige* Oil Spill

The environmental harm caused by *Prestige*'s toxic heavy
fuel oil cargo began within hours (36 hours, according to the
BMA) of the initial rupture, and persisted with decreasing egress
from the sunken hull for up to two years. This makes it, along with
uncapped the blow-out of the oil rig *Ixtoc 1* off Mexico in 1979,
the release of 460 million gallons of crude by Iraq in 1991, and
Amoco Cadiz's loss of 223,000 tons on France's coast in 1978, one
of the longest-running pollution incidents in tanker history.
Prestige would also come in as the fifth-worst among actual tanker
spills (behind *Amoco Cadiz, Aegean Captain, Braer (86,000 tons),
Castillo de Bellver* (252,000 tons off South Africa, 1983), and
roughly tied with *Sea Empress* (72,000 tons, 1996) (ITOPF, 2005).

Though the environmental impact is still being felt, these
figures provide a snapshot:

> In mid-December [2002] the Spanish
> government suspended fishing from the Costa da Morte
> to the French border; by early January, 654 of northern
> Spain's 1,064 beaches were splotched with crude.
> Ninety thousand fishermen faced financial ruin. …the
> Spanish government quickly agreed to pay US$42 per
> day, as long as fishing was prohibited… One fisherman
> in Laxe described the compensation at '*una maravilla*'
> given that it exceeded the money many would have
> made on the job and that it came during the winters
> months, when catches would have been low in any
> case, owing to bad weather. This *maravilla* lasted 120
> days.
>
> Nowhere in Europe does fishing matter more
> than in Spain, where some 120,000 fishermen sailing
> 20,000 boats bring in 1.1 million tons of fish per year,

mainly mackerel, bonito, hake and anchovy. The
Prestige disaster turned [Galicia] into ground zero of
the *marea negra* ('black tide'). [A local fisherman]
described 'seas churning black with *chapapluma*, the
colloquial term for the mix of oil and dead seabirds.' As
many as 250,000 birds have died. "We are living off
social security and crying a lot," he said. A scientist
opined that "contamination has occurred on the
molecular level in the sand, sea and vegetation, and it's
entering the food chain" (Tayler, 2004, 82-85).

In terms of financial fallout for the region, by
March 2004, a year ago,

The *Prestige* had cost European taxpayers $1.16
billion, of that, the autonomous region of Galicia alone
has spent $140 million. The total cost for Europe may
run as high as $2.89 billion, far exceeding the $2 billion
that *Exxon Valdez* spill cost. Given that the *Prestige*
was the third tanker to go down on the Costa Da Morte
in the past 26 years, one might expect that the Spanish
would have an emergency plan in place. But they don't.
The government initially played down the effects of the
disaster, relying for some weeks on volunteers to clean
up the mess before mobilizing its troops. 'Spain has the
human resources and technology. If they were
organized, they could have confronted the problem and
provided an adequate response. But there is no will'
(Tayler, 2004, 80-85).

The *Prestige*'s flag-state, the Bahamas Maritime Authority,
had this to say about the casualty, its aftermath, and Spain's
response. This was delivered to the IMO and posted in their
literature. It seems, in many ways, addressed to Spain.

Prestige was a tragedy that should have been avoided. The name *Prestige* will go down in history alongside major shipping casualties, such as *Erika*. Although *Prestige* was a 26-year-old tanker, all the evidence indicates that the vessel was well managed and maintained. The failure of the coastal state to offer assistance or respond positively to the request by professional salvors to provide a place of refuge was to have dire consequences. The response of some European states has been disappointing

At an early stage, the BMA sent two of its senior staff members to Spain to offer assistance, and to gather evidence. Unfortunately, the country's cooperation, which might have been expected in such circumstances, has not been forthcoming. BMA is proceeding with it's independent investigation and has received full cooperation and access to the vessel's records from the [ABS]. The BMA has retained the services of experts in the field of structural failures to assist in its assessment of the evidence. All those involved in shipping regret such incidents as the *Prestige*, since they lead to bad publicity for the whole industry. It would be naïve to think that such accidents will not happen again, or that double-hulled vessels will solve the problem (BMA, 2003, 1).

Technological Innovation in *Prestige* Aftermath

The *Prestige* came to rest at latitude 42 degrees, 15 minutes north by longitude 12 degrees, 08 minutes west. Spain tasked the French sub *Nautilus* to monitor the site pretty much continuously. So began the most technologically ambitious oil- recovery effort ever attempted, to recover the remaining 15,000 or so tons of fuel oil from almost three miles deep. As supported by the several articles cited from professional journals (Tayler, 2004, and Tyler,

2005), the methods used to extract oil from and seal the hull of the *Prestige* over two years were both ground-breaking and standard-setting. This is borne out by the fact that the whole first summer season was spent basically ironing out and devising technological solutions to a very complex problem. Prototypes were invented, tested, and either passed or failed. Companies and technologies were founded and marketed on the equipment used, or went bust. It is the deepest attempt since the sub *Kursk* salvage, 2001.

The Spanish government, to its credit, harnessed a wealth of academic and scientific brain-trust to constantly predict ocean current patterns, and try to anticipate where the oil from *Prestige* would go and when. "The Spanish government appointed a scientific advisory committee, which recommended pumping the fuel out of the wreck [or] covering it. Spanish universities and institutions worked on studies of the area of the wreck to determine its geology and provide wind, wave and current information" (Tyler, 2005, 55-56). One of the support team in this endeavor was a University of Rhode Island visiting student, Dr. Eric Comerma, a PhD graduate of the Universidad Politechnica de Cataluna in Spain, where he specializes as a civil engineer in simulated pollution distribution. He is presently working on ocean current analysis for the Spanish government, to enable them to better anticipate outcomes of casualties like the *Prestige*.

Figure 8, following page, illustrates some of the scatter effect from the *Prestige* during the first year of the spill. This is prepared by the French oil pollution watchdog CEDRE, which was formed on the heels of the *Amoco Cadiz* disaster off the French coast in 1978, during which there were no tugs powerful enough to pull the laden VLCC from danger, resulting in France's worst oil tanker spill (Hamon, 2003). It is possible to see that *Prestige*'s oil migrated as far as the inner reaches of the English Channel and the Channel Islands. Very strong currents and tides in the region may have helped to distribute the floating oil to wide swathes of otherwise difficult-to-access coastline.

The physical disposal of sludgy oil from beaches, sea surfaces, and the rocky coast presented persistent problems – especially since up to 140 tons a day continued to egress from the ruptured hull. These reminders floated several miles from *Prestige*'s grave to the ocean's surface. One creative solution – to recycle, repackage and resell the oil, shows the kind of lateral thinking, which enabled salvors and scientists to coordinate extraction of the oil from the hull.

The *Prestige* salvage has undoubtedly set a technological standard.

> Treatment of the hydrocarbons brought up from the wreck is scheduled [at] Repsol YPF. "The stuff is very poor quality (but) could be sold." Recycling 90,500 tons of fuel residue mixed in with sand from more than 1,000 beaches whose biodiversity was massively damaged in the disaster will also be a laborious process. Some 70,000 tons have been placed in waterproof ditches. Th[e] process could last until end 2006.
>
> Spain has also asked the International Oil Pollution Compensation Fund to stump up some 514 million Euros towards the clean-up cost and 120 million more for the pumping operation. Madrid has also demanded from the ABS, which was responsible for certifying the vessel's seaworthiness, one billion dollars compensation. (Nov. 2004) About 95 percent of what was on board has been recovered. The remaining five percent adhered to the inside of the hull (Lloyd's Agency, 2005, 2).

The extraction of oil from the sunken hull of the *Prestige* is still admired as the most technologically advanced treatment of its kind.

In the summer and fall of 2004, 14,880 tons of heavy crude oil were removed from the wreck of the

tanker *Prestige*, lying at a depth of 12,600 feet. This operation marks the greatest depths at which oil has ever been removed from a wreck. The techniques and tools had to be created by the companies involved: Repsol [and] Sonsub. The Spanish government spent about $130 million on this project. Challenges included the water depth, accessing the fuel with in the tanks, getting the fuel oil to move into the system used to bring it back to the surface, then actually transferring the fuel. The French Research Institute plug[ged] leaks in the wreck [Dec 2002-Feb.2003]. Leakage was reduced from 143 tons daily to about 2.4 tons. The major challenge was the extreme viscosity of the oil at this depth. Due to the high pressure and a water temperature of 36.6 degrees F, the fuel oil had reached a state known as *pseudo-plastic*. 'If you took a glass full of oil at that viscosity and you lay it sideways on the table, at the end of [an] our we'd see a slight budge.' The hole in the hull had to be at least 27.6 inches in diameter for the gravity-feed method to work (Tyler, 2005, 55-56).

The technology used was more than ground-breaking, it was ocean-penetrating:

The development of an [unmanned] hot tapping machine to operate at this depth is also a world first, according to Repsol YPF. Sonsub inserted 56-foot long pipes into the tanks, so water would replace oil coming out and maintain the oil's flow. An ultrasonic beam detection system was adapted to determine the fuel level in the tanks. 66,000-gallon bags could not operate with doors open in sea states about five. Five aluminum shuttle tanks were constructed. Each was 75.5 feet long and 17 feet in diameter, and could carry 92,460 gallons of oil. In rough seas the shuttles were unloaded underwater at a depth of about 164 feet. After the oil was removed, nutrients were injected into the wreck to speed the rate at which naturally occurring microorganisms would transform the toxic compounds through decomposition, converting them into carbon dioxide and water (Tyler, 2005, 55-56).

The *Prestige* spill contributed greatly to the understanding of oil extraction at depth. This statement is fully supported, at least in the context of commercial salvage. There is little doubt that the navies of the world have made considerable advances at extraction of valuable or harmful cargoes from deep depths. Precedents include location of US Navy submarines *Squalus*, NH, October 1939, *Thresher,* off Cape Cod, April 1963, and *Scorpion,* off Azores, May 1968. The more recent recovery of a nuclear warhead extricated from the Mediterranean and salvage of the Russian nuclear submarine *Kursk*, off Murmansk, in May, 2001 are other examples. Whether the objects sought have been human lives, technology, valuable cargo (*USS Central America, USS Republic, Atocha*), or historically significant wrecks (*Titanic, Bismark, PT-109*), there have been many milestones of deep-sea extraction before the *Prestige*. However by all accounts the specific oil pollution mitigation techniques, at such staggering depths and temperatures (12,000 feet and very cold temperatures in which to extract congealed crude oil), were truly groundbreaking. Perhaps this line of work can serve as another arrow in the quiver of opportunities that the ISU pursues; several of their members have turned to wreck removal, for clearing channels or recycling old, strong steel, to supplement their incomes.

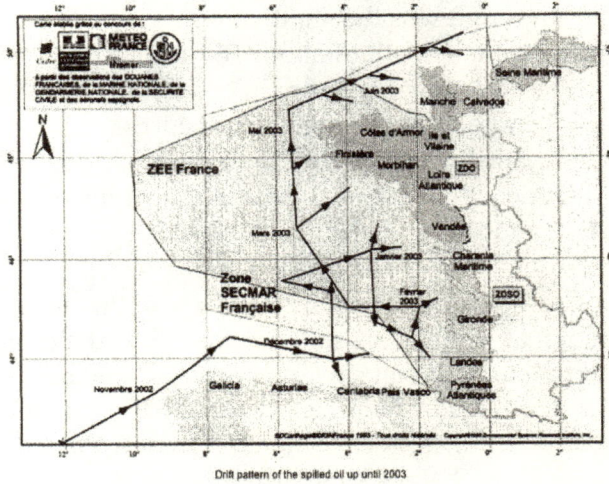

Drift pattern of the spilled oil up until 2003

FIGURE 8:
MAP SHOWING DRIFT PATTERN OF *PRESTIGE* OIL,
2003
Source: CEDRE, (2005); www.le-cedre.fr/uk/spill/prestige.html

Perhaps the postscript the *Prestige* will have (in the otherwise near-empty credit box), will be the recovery's extraordinary contribution to scientific salvage technology.

Prestige Oil Spill Compared with *Erika* Oil Spill, 1999

Langewiesche specifically details the seminal *Erika* disaster. Because no LOF was signed before the ship sank, as *Erika* was proceeding under its own steam for the coast, with cooperation from French authorities, who were not denying it a place of refuge, Lloyd's List, 2003j), most accounts of the mishap occur in the regular press.

In December 1999, Europe experienced an accident that was similar in political impact to that of the *Exxon Valdez*. It was the loss of the smallish tanker *Erika*, nominally Maltese, that was owned by a single-ship shell company, inspected by the Italian classification society, RINA, and manned by an underpaid and beleaguered Indian crew. Though it was twenty five years old, it had been chartered by the French company Total Fina to carry [26,000 to 31,000, figures vary] tons of sludge-like fuel oil from Dunkirk.

In a storm off Southern Brittany, having developed a leak and a list, it broke in two in international waters while running for refuge toward the mouth of the Loire. The crew was rescued un-injured, but both sections of the hull sank, releasing gooey black masses that rode beneath the ocean's surface as well as on it and, after drifting for about a week, began to hit the French beaches in noxious waves that drove France and its neighbors into an uproar. The captain was jailed in France for more than a week. Upon his release he said that the *Erika*'s condition had been poor, and that ...the ship's management company, had instructed him to run south for Spain after the ship's hull had started to crack. Tracked down by Lloyd's List in

London, [the owner stated that] "There is no doubt that everything was done according to the rules." But that was precisely the problem over the previous two years the ship had successfully gone through four port-state inspection. (2004, 93-97).

Ironically, the *Erika* hull failure was due to structural weakness compounded by storms. Figure 9, following page, maps *Erika*'s initial oil spill. With characteristic color, Langewiesche describes the *Prestige*'s demise and gives a mere snapshot of the public clamor that the oil pollution ignited:

> A replay of the *Erika* occurred as once again an old tanker had come apart in a storm. *Prestige*; it flew the Bahamian flag and had a Greek captain and a Filipino and Romanian crew. It was passing by in international waters when it sprang a leak and began to list. The captain radioed for help and turned for La Coruna and the protection of its harbor. The Spanish authorities refused it shelter, and, under the guns of their warships, forced it back to sea. It was a cowardly act, a sign of governmental impotence and frustration.
> For five days the *Prestige* fought a losing battle offshore, wandering slowly, being battered to death by the storm. The crew was rescued. When finally the ship could endure no more, it did not simply bleed into La Coruna's harbor as it might have done, but broke in two and blew the filth of the world all over the coast of Portugal, France and Spain. In Finisterre now, people were marching in massive and angry demonstrations. They demanded the government resign, and they sprayed signs on buildings reading NUNCA MAS! [No more] (Langewiesche, 2004, 98-99).

The dramatic wrecks of *Prestige* and *Erika*, so close together both temporally and geographically, despoiled a vast portion of the immense Bay of Biscay. Together they have left an indelible imprint on the minds and memories of a generation of French, Spanish and European citizens and legislators. Indeed, these two casualties have served as a form of clarion call to action, which the IMO, the government of Spain, the EC and EU have responded to, pushing through and testing various legislative schemes and contractual amendments. As the cleanup from these spills winds up and participants wend their way to and through court, the resolutions born of the *Erika* and *Prestige* disasters emerge from the anvil of debate and undergo tempering to determine relative strengths.

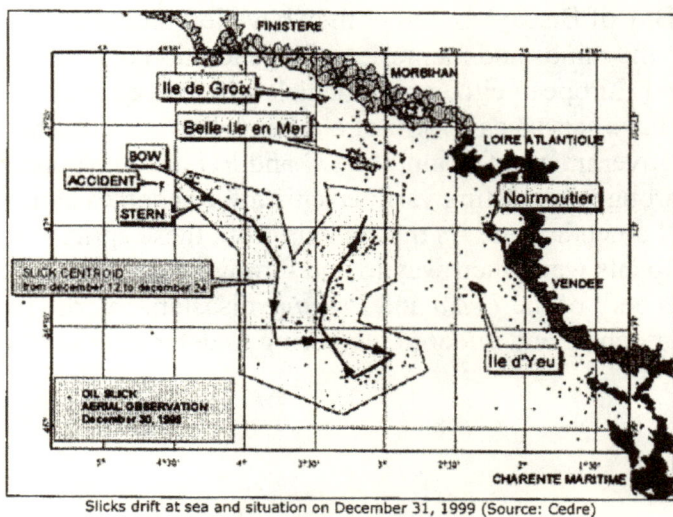

Slicks drift at sea and situation on December 31, 1999 (Source: Cedre)

FIGURE 9:
MAP SHOWING SITE OF MT *ERIKA* SINKING AND
SPILL, 1999
Source: CEDRE, (2005); www.le-cedre.fr/uk/spill/erika.html

CHAPTER 7

IMO'S PLACES OF REFUGE RESOLUTION

Erika, Castor, and *Prestige*: *Force Majeure* Versus Places of Refuge

The IMO drafters point out that, in issuing their resolution, they are rewriting maritime and Admiralty law, adding to the lexicon, and spackling a legal gap between *force majeure* and pure salvage, even salvage modified by SCOPIC. "There have been serious discussions on the provision of Places of Refuge. This is the agreed term for what have previously been known as Port of Refuge, Safe Haven, and the like. The probable outcome is a test of guidelines of the Master of the ship seeking refuge and for the coastal state in which the ship is looking for a safe place to shelter. The problems of sovereignty will prevent a mandatory approach to the issue" (IMO News, 2002, 18).

It will help to at least briefly define and explain *force majeure*. It is

> A doctrine of international law which conveys limited legal immunity upon vessels that are forced to seek refuge or repairs within the jurisdiction of another nation due to uncontrollable external force it prohibits coastal state enforcement of its laws breached due to the vessel's entry. The strict definition is an overwhelming force or condition of such severity that it threatens loss of the vessel, cargo, or crew, unless immediate corrective action is taken. [under which a] vessel should be excused from compliance with domestic laws which prohibit such entry (USCG, 2002, 4, and CMI, 2002, 30).

The burden of proof rests with the Master, owner, and vessel to prove that *force majeure* applied to the facts of each case.

The target of this IMO Resolution, signed by 111 nations as of April 2005, is not the traditional casualty shipwreck containing personnel. There is no doubt that countries, even Spain (*Castor*), are required to, and would, expend their utmost resources towards the saving of human life imperiled on the sea. The absence of crew on board distinguishes casualties such as *Castor* and *Prestige* from the standard *force majeure* model of yore, a point which IMO makes clear: "The Assembly adopted guidelines on places of refuge for ships in need of assistance. These guidelines are intended for use when the safety of life is not involved" (IMO, 2004b, 2).

In contrast, IMO defines places of refuge as "an aspect of contingency planning in the consideration of which the rights and interests of coastal states, as well as the need to render assistance to vessels that are damaged or disabled or otherwise in distress at sea, ought to be taken into account. In November 2003, the IMO Assembly adopted two resolutions - an important step in assisting those involved in incidents that may lead to the need for a place of refuge to make the right decisions at the right time" (IMO, 2005b). The first of these resolutions, Places of Refuge, was: "intended for use when a ship has suffered an incident, the best way of preventing damage or pollution from its progressive deterioration is to transfer its cargo and bunkers, and to repair the casualty" (IMO, 2005).

IMO recognizes the inevitable political aspect of this kind of public decision:

> To bring such a ship into a place of refuge near a coast may endanger the coastal state, both economically, and from the environmental point of view. Local authorities and populations may strongly object to the operation. Granting access to

a place of refuge could involve a political decision
which can only be taken on a case-by-case basis.
Consideration would need to be given to balancing
the interests of the affected ship with those of the
environment (IMO, 2005, 4).

IMO candidly recognizes the influence of the *Erika*, *Castor*
and *Prestige* in the evolution and expedition of their policy goals
regarding places of refuge. Real action on the resolution began in
earnest "in December 2000, in response to the *Erika* incident of
December 1999. Further urgency to the work came in the
aftermath of the incident involving the fully laden tanker *Castor*"
(IMO, 2005).

In early 2001 IMO [recognized] that the time had come
for the Organization to undertake, as a matter of priority, a
global consideration of the problem of places of refuge for
disabled vessels, and adopt any measures required to ensure
that, in the interests of safety of life at sea and
environmental protection, coastal states reviewed their
contingency arrangements so that such ships are provided
with assistance and facilities as might be required in the
circumstances. The November 2002 sinking of the *Prestige*
further highlighted the issue (IMO, 2005).

IMO recognized that the Places of Refuge would be a
thorny issue and that any resolution was unlikely to please all of
the parties. Yet, perhaps bolstered by the resolve of then-Secretary
O'Neill, who reigned for 14 years at the post, IMO did not flinch,
and passed the Resolution quickly. Addressing the problem in
general, almost laymen terms, IMO authors observe that:

Ships with structural damage and a dirty or
volatile cargo in their tanks are not among the most
welcomed visitors in the coastal waters of any state.
There is little point in attempting to apportion blame on

those who have made decisions to keep stricken ships away from their coastlines. Nonetheless, in some cases, a refusal could result in compounding the problem, which may ultimately result in endangering life, the ship and the environment during the debate on places of refuge, the question was asked whether a coastal state is under an obligation, or at least is not precluded, under international law, from providing a place [of refuge], in order to remove the ship from the threat of danger and undertake repairs or otherwise deal with the situations.

International law recognizes the right of states to regulate entry into their ports (UNCLOS, Article 2, refers to the sovereignty of a coastal State over its land territory, internal waters, archipelagic waters and the territorial sea). The right of a foreign ship to stop and anchor in case of *force majeure* or distress is explicitly referred to by UNCLOS.

The right of a foreign ship to enter a port or internal waters of another State in situations of *force majeure* or distress is not regulated by UNCLOS, although this constitutes an internationally accepted practice, at least in order to preserve human life. This, however, does not preclude the adoption of rules or guidelines complementing the provisions of UNCLOS. Meanwhile, the right of a coastal State to take action to protect its coastline from marine pollution is well established in international law. Relevant provisions include: UNCLOS, Articles 194, 195, 198, 199, 211, 221, 225; Salvage Convention, Article 9; and Facilitation Convention Article V(2) (IMO, 2005, and Von Glahn, 1996).

Both existing and proposed refuge solutions have come up against *de facto* law – laws of common practice and usage (as opposed to *de jure* law, which is court-decreed, Von Glahn, 1996). These oft-unwritten codes of practice can be difficult to break.

Tanker Disasters / Eric T. Wiberg

Under longstanding maritime tradition and the practice of good seamanship, the master of a ship faced with a serious emergency is expected to seek shelter to avoid disaster. To some extent the practice is codified in the revised Chapter V of SOLAS, which requires that the owner, the charterer, or the company operating the ship or any other person, shall not prevent or restrict the master of the ship from taking or executing any decision which, in the master's professional judgment, is necessary for safe navigation and protection of the marine environment.

Similarly, SOLAS Article IV provides that ships which are not subject to the provisions of the Convention at the time of their departure on any voyage, shall not become subject to the provisions of the Convention on account of any deviation from their intended voyage due to stress of weather or any other case of *force majeure*. The duty to render assistance to vessels and persons in distress at sea is a well-established principle of international maritime law (Article 98 of UNCLOS) and SOLAS regulation V/7 requires governments to ensure that any necessary arrangements are made for distress communication and coordination in their area of responsibility and for the rescue of persons in distress at sea round their coasts. These arrangements shall include search and rescue, having regard to the density of the seagoing traffic and the navigational dangers.

By focusing more on human life and safety rather than on what is to be done with the ship in cases of *force majeure* or distress, these provisions do not of themselves give a right of entry to a place of refuge, nor do they explicitly refer to the question of a coastal State's obligation to establish places of refuge. On the other hand, neither do they preclude such a principle (IMO, 2005c).

It is apparent that drafters of the Places of Refuge Resolution were painfully aware of their need to recognize and skirt all manner of political and legal pitfalls. "Given this background, it has proved possible for IMO to develop the Guidelines on Places of Refuge ..in a manner which retains a proper and equitable balance between the rights and interests of coastal States and the need to render assistance to ships which are damaged or disabled or otherwise in distress at sea" (IMO, 2005c, 2).

It is a fact, as shown in the *Prestige* case, that when all of the crew had been evacuated from a vessel, the operation to save the ship is no longer of a search and rescue (SAR) nature, but becomes relegated to pure property salvage and damage mitigation. This is more stark when the vessel no longer has its own propulsion, and must rely on a tow. In the *Prestige* case, it is debatable whether in the first stages the vessel was fully without its own motive power. The Master and crew were ordered off the ship, while the machinery could still have been manipulated. With the *Castor*, once the crew had been evacuated, the Spanish authorities felt that their job was done, and from that time onwards the problem was purely one for salvors and shipowners.

In all of these cases, including the *Braer*, where the crew had been lifted off of the ship, *force majeure* no longer applied(the author worked for the company, B&H Oceans, which lost the *Braer* and was privy not only to the U.K. DOT report, but first-hand accounts by the Superintendent Engineer, Mr. Quameral Khan, a survivor). *Force majeure* mainly applies to ships under their own steam, on which are living breathing crew members who wish to use the ship to save themselves, the vessel, and cargo.

Obviously a lot more leniency will be given by coastal states to a manned ship than to an unmanned one. For this reason, the question of if - and when - to abandon ship is a particularly important one to those on the shipowning side. Salvors have created a middle ground by actually placing salvage masters and crew on board ships, as they did on *Prestige* and *Castor*. However, they are generally deemed to have taken responsibility themselves for extricating those they put aboard (Mowat, 1958, and ISU 2005).

Though it is a stick in the bundle of possible rights, and has a strong emotive appeal based in centuries of humanity and the traditions of the sea, *force majeure* as a legal principle is superceded where the men can be or have been safely evacuated. The rescue then becomes a salvage, some of the time constraints may be eased. The focus, in the case of tankers, shifts to supporting the tugs and salvage crews, and, ultimately, to seeking and ideally securing a place of refuge at which to repair the vessel and offload the cargo. Holding out for *force majeure,* at the peril of the lives of those on board, however, is unacceptable, particularly in the safety-conscious culture of the ISM Code (International Safety Management); a rigidly standardized set of safety rules implemented in the mid 1990s.

In its conclusion, while recognizing the limitations of a resolution which is not strictly enforceable, i.e. is not affirmative law imposing a strict duty, the IMO notes that:

> It would be highly desirable if, taking the IMO Guidelines into account, coastal states designated places of refuge for use when confronted with situations involving ships (laden tankers in particular) in need of assistance off their coasts and, accordingly, drew up relevant emergency plans, instead of being unprepared to face such situations and, because of that, risking the wrong decision being made by improvising or, in the heat of the moment, acting under pressure from groups representing various interests (IMO, 2005).

While the *Castor* case made it to arbitration, and has been to a large extent fully litigated, the *Prestige* incident has not yet led to major legal cases of the type that can be seen as conclusive regarding liability and cost-apportionment. The IMO Resolution has evidently moved faster than the courts of law. It is worth considering that the final, conclusive cases emanating from the 1989 *Exxon Valdez* spill was not issued until 2001 – some twelve years later. The Spain v. ABS case, begun last year, is still in the jurisdictional phase; jurists are not tackling the substantive issues yet.

Realistically, it will probably be another decade until all aspects of the *Prestige* damages have been litigated, arbitrated, or settled, even bearing in mind that in general European citizenry are far less litigious than their counterparts in the U.S.. For this reason, the IMO Resolution, inasmuch as it was almost certainly influenced by both the *Erika, Castor* and *Prestige* incidents, is the most universal resource available for trying to control the effects of each spill.

Influence of *Erika*, *Castor*, and *Prestige* Incidents on the IMO Resolution

Political Support for IMO's Resolution

Trying pointedly to be circumspect, the ISU published this overall analysis of the relationship between different parties; salvage master, coastal state, and SOSREP or equivalent:

> It would be wrong to suggest that every marine casualty is treated like a leper of the seas. It would be unjust to suggest that authorities ashore are interested only in ensuring the unwanted ship stays as far as possible from their coast, in the hope that it will eventually become someone else's problem. The salvor now expects to have to justify his request for a safe haven. He must be prepared for some tough negotiations. At the same time, he will obey the instructions of the coastal state. If ordered to take a ship out, he will comply. He has no choice, even if the refusal to grant shelter condemns the ship. This is entirely proper, as permission to enter a place of

refuge is a matter solely for the coastal state
concerned. It is the sovereign right of that state to take
this crucial decision (Timmermans, 2004b, 7).

The conciliatory opening tone of this ISU missive is
perhaps misleading. In truth, there is little conciliatory between the
ISU and Spain following that country's recent crackdown on
crippled ships using pecuniary punishment. A confrontation seems
to have been made inevitable by the ISU's and IMO's bullying of
the European Commission, and the Spaniards' insistence on
sovereignty at any price. Yet Spain is hardly alone...

In terms of coastal protection, the equivalent of Britain's
SOSREP, for Secretary of State's Representative, in France is the
Maritime Prefect and in Germany the position is called the Central
Accident Command. "Only the U.K. has a system under which a
senior official, the SOSREP, is free of political interference to
place the national interest above that of local or regional interests.
A minister may not intervene whilst a salvage operation is in
progress. Other jurisdictions [read: Spain], however, continue to
place greater emphasis on political intervention. The harbormaster
is in a position analogous to that of the salvage master. Both can
expect to come under extreme pressure in a major casualty -
especially when pollution threatens. Both have to take account of
the political, operational realities of the situation, yet endeavor to
implement sensible decisions" (Timmermans, 2004b, 6).

This unflappable authority was demonstrated amply in the
case of the *Tarpenbek* in 1979. Following a channel collision, the
SOSREP invited the ship to run up on a beach on posh Isle of
Wight, to which the local summer residents vehemently objected.
The ship beached, its bunkers were lightered, salvage tugs pulled it
off the beach, and it was towed to Europe. It is hard to imagine
many other non-military contexts where a representative has such
authority. It is as though the SOSREP himself acts covered by
force majeure.

Leading by example, "The U.K. SOSREP noted that
neighboring coastal states should cooperate in identifying the best

141

refuge for casualties. He maintained that governments should be prepared to accept a casualty if the best refuge is in their jurisdiction, even if the accident happens in a neighboring jurisdiction. In contrast, the Spanish Government's Royal Decree appears to be designed to deter requests for shelter. It also leaves no room for constructive cooperation with neighboring states" (Timmermans, 2004a, 4). And yet the problem of cooperation between the ISU, Spain, and the IMO has not gotten better – relations have crystallized and are rapidly calcifying. The problem seems to have gotten worse. Whether IMO's Places of Refuge Resolution alleviates the situation remains to be seen.

A lot of the concern for progress is based on pragmatic recognition of the powerful role that politics plays in many of the Places of Refuge decisions. "The real problem is associated with publicizing these locations. Naturally, there is a political price to be paid when such locations are disclosed. Coastal communities in the front line tend to argue, with some force, that the safe haven should be in someone else backyard" (ISU, 2005d, 6). The then-ISU President in 2004 observed :

> I have sympathy with the harbormaster faced with an imminent threat of catastrophic pollution. He may well be caught up in a tangled web of vested interests, while struggling to reconcile political pressure and operational realities. The solution is to adopt a strategy creating a new climate of confidence. Coastal communities providing places of refuge do so in the national interest. They need the comfort of knowing that funds have been set aside for clean-up and compensation, should pollution result from a decision to grant shelter.
>
> In fact, governments should go further and *proactively reward* coastal communities accepting this burden in the national interest. This would transform attitudes. It would establish a new and

more positive platform for cooperation between
salvors, port authorities and other shore-based
interests. An efficient compensation system, backed
by community reward would motivate people. The
funds required for initiatives of this type are modest
in relation to the billion-Euro-plus costs arising
from a single *Prestige*-type event. This approach
should be considered at the EU level, as it addresses
a pan-European problem (Timmermans, 2004b, 4).

The ISU had the following suggestions as to how to
anticipate such casualties and ameliorate the environmental
damage: "Rather than searching for scapegoats and putting people
in prison, it is more constructive to identify the key lessons from
the *Prestige*. The obvious lessons ((ISU, 2004l, 7, condensed by
the author) include:

1. Salvage is a preventive strategy far more cost-effective than
   clean-up, compensation.
2. New requirements on the tanker industry represent a quick-
   fix and are no panacea.
3. Coastal States need to value salvage as a preventive tool
   [and] support salvors. 4. Action should be taken to reduce
   the political content of casualty management.
4. Focus on the Best Environmental Option, methodical risk
   assessment, prompt action.
5. A request for a safe haven should be refused only if an
   alternative course of action is identified as the Best
   Environmental Option.
6. Naturally, risk-assessment should take account of the
   potential consequences of refusal.
7. The trend towards criminalization of spill events should be
   nipped in the bud. At its worst, owners and managers may
   conclude that they cannot ask their technical teams to
   attend on scene. This trend may also deter the expertise
   needed to prevent a spill.

8. There is a need for radical thinking on places of refuge. The time is ripe for new ideas on compensation, should the entry of a casualty into a safe haven result in pollution.

It is perhaps not surprising that one of the most consistently strident voices on the floor of the IMO Places of Refuge debate is that of the salvors, who have developed intimate technical knowledge of the reality of such operations, the risks and possible rewards, and the essentials of timing. While SOSREPs or their equivalent are presumably navy-trained or experience in some way with ship-casualty operations, it must be frustrating for the salvors to take orders from different coastal state's ministers. Yet respect is due to the often involuntary host of these spills; the coordinator who may be left with a lasting environmental and political legacy of despoilment by pollution. Their perspective follows.

Counter-Arguments Against IMO's Resolution

In February of 2004, Spain pushed through legislation making it a crime punishable by severe fines of up to tens of millions of Euros, to bring in a damaged ship leaking toxins harmful to the environment to their shores. This law, known as a Royal Decree, operates not only independently of *force majeure* and contrary to the new IMO Places of Refuge Resolution; it was almost certainly drafted, temporally, in relation to the *Erika, Castor* and *Prestige* incidents, as a direct counterpoint to the Resolution. The response, as can be imagined, was strident. At the same time a cooperative IMO agreement was being hammered out (some, like Langewiesche (2004) might suggest shoe-horned), the Spanish were going the other direction; hardening up their response in anticipation of more *Prestige*-like disasters.

There are, of course, counter-arguments and alternatives being offered for the IMO Places of Refuge Resolution. Most of them have been contested, some by the IMO itself, and none of them have yet to be rigorously tested. The main proponents and critics of the Places of Refuge Resolution have been the governments of coastal states such as Spain, which have tabled – and passed – their own, sovereign, counter-measures, complete with stiff fines. To illustrate this point, it is calculated that if Spain's Royal Decree had been in effect at the time the *Prestige* approached Finisterre in need of assistance, the bond which Spain would have required the owners to pay would have been US$522 million, in the form of a financial guarantee.

Half a billon U.S. dollars, to most, is an insurmountable expense; an un-payable liquid asset on top of the hefty annual dues and pool payouts, which vessel owners already pay to be members of P&I Clubs, and to meet their financial responsibilities for oil pollution liabilities under a number of other international protocols. The amount slides from being onerous to being usurious. Recall the case studies of *Protokletas*, the laden Panamax bulker that was held outside Angra Dos Rias Brazil for nine months in 1992, before the owner decided it would be cheaper to scuttle ship and cargo, or the *Smirdan*, which was told to pay US$10 million bond to enter Singapore in 1997, could not, waited with cargo for three years, and ultimately sold ship and cargo for one percent of its value, or the *Ventura*, denied access to Colombo, Sri Lanka until a monsoon claimed ship and cargo, worth US$2 million, at anchorage.

Another reform camp, which has its feet firmly with the coastal state, and not with the floating pariahs, is the European Commission. In the flurry of legislative activity following quickly on the heels of the *Erika*, *Castor* and *Prestige* incidents, three separate *Erika* Packages have been proposed to reform the standard of tankers permitted to enter European waters, and to track and police those that do. The right to refuse any ship a place of refuge is steadfastly guarded. Though there have been politicized attacks on a number of the proposals, and subsequently some trimming, overall the EC is making strides towards better protecting the European coastline. Spain sequestered for itself its own corner and a superior law, the Royal Decree which is tantamount in Spanish waters. Doubtless Spain is interested in testing (results for far are roughly 50/50 – one ship rejected; a container, or box ship, another granted refuge; surprisingly an LPG tanker, both within two months of one another, in 2004.

In a popular recent book essentially attacking the shipping industry for its obfuscations, journalist and author William Langewiesche (2004) offers an unflattering depiction of the IMO as being in close cahoots with the very shipowners they were tasked by the U.N. in the 1950s with regulating. The book itself, subtitled The Outlaw Sea: A World of Freedom, Chaos, and Crime, serves as a form of long Op/Ed piece or diatribe against the shipping industry and those who regulate it; though his opinions are passionate, and not always fully informed, balanced reportage requires a counter opinion.

> In the 1980s, ships flying flags of convenience began to predominate at sea, the 'open registries' upon which the [flagging] system was based mounted a *coup d'etat* at the IMO and effectively seized control. Those registries were nothing more than proxy nations in the hands of the global shipping industry. Because the IMO is funded by membership fees based on the size from the respective fleets, they were by then also proving most of the organization's financial support, and so they were able to demand access, denied to them before, to the technical committees where new standards were decided upon and where the real power lay.... The IMO had been captured by the very forces it had sought to regulate (Langewiesche, 2004, 87-88).

The French in particular led the way, through the European Commission, towards reform. As the primary victims of the *Erika* damages, perhaps it is meet that they did. Already, as at 2004, two of the three packages of reforms had passed in modified form. (Fairplay, 2004c). And other port-states and coastal states are noticing. Southeast Asian shipowners have protested Europe's new stringency, and the U.S. legislators are aware that they may be eclipsed by Europe for phaseouts like single hulls (CMA, 2004).

Photos of the *Erika*, stern-up, nose-diving to the sea floor through a mire of oil were smeared across the covers of dozens of major international publications. While there is little or no photographic evidence of many oil spills, and tanker spills only account for between three and twelve percent of the oil which enters the planet's waterways (ITOPF, 2005, and Intertanko, 2005), the *Erika* sinking was truly a photogenic and dramatic episode; a *femme fatale* caught on film. The public was appalled, livid, and fascinated. They didn't want to see any more *Erika*'s on their shores, and were willing to pressure politicians to go to the highest levels in order to amend the rules. Indirectly, the *Erika* disaster led to an accelerated ban of single-hull tankers in Europe, and to faster implementation of double-hull technology worldwide (CMA, 2004). But, for all the bombast and political posturing, little progress was made in the form of Places of Refuge, or outlawing of tankers like *Erika* by the European Commission. According to Langewiesche, IMO had a direct hand in cutting down the Commission's efforts

> The French, who were the angriest [after the *Erika*], clearly understood the limitations of their geographic circumstances as compared to those of the U.S.. They realized that any imposition of new standard by France alone could have little effect on the parade of unsafe ships in the international waters off their shores. The solution was regional action, specifically through the newly assertive executive branch of the European Union, the European Commission.
> Confident in the support of Europe's vast environmentalist constituency, the[y] took up the cause and proposed aggressive maritime reforms. However the IMO fought back: privately it accused the European Commission of technical ignorance and cheap political grandstanding. In France, it was now understood that

ship inspections had taken on the importance of national defense (Langewiesche, 2004, 93-97).

France's response to these three casualties can best be described as cooperative reform. France has consistently coordinated with other neighboring states and worked up an effective lobby or bloc of voters in favor of their packages. This is something that Spain failed to do, mustering only Mexico, Dominica, and Argentina for a reform bill which they saw as particularly important to justifying their later Royal Decree in 2004.

While visiting the site of the *Prestige* spill in Galicia, Tayler ruminates:

> I wondered how the Spanish government could have even considered sending a damaged vessel such as the *Prestige* though these turbulent seas. There is a push to establish well-designated ports of refuge for leaking ships, despite resistance in many local communicates. IMO has in fact agreed to harmonize what have been notoriously inconsistent certification standards Environmentalists are pressing for the current ceiling on damages ($290 million) to be abolished but shipping companies and countries with strong maritime interest are hampering the pace of reforms. Jose-Maria Aznar, the Spanish prime minister, declared in May 2003 that the *Prestige* disaster was 'something well and truly past' (Tayler, 2004, 85).

In fact, the Prestige spill did not stop returning oil to its sender, Spain, for another year. By that time, Aznar had paid the ultimate political price; he was voted out of power.

Detention of *Prestige*'s Captain, Criminalization of Crew

Meanwhile, almost as a side-show to the cleanup, the detention of the ship's Master continued. His fate symbolized that of shipowners and regulators trying to weave their way along the Spanish coast, trying not to become entangled in their new, restrictive net of regulations. In September of 2003, ten months after the spill (recall, he was arrested the day he left his ship), this was the update;

> Lawyers acting for Apostolos Mangouras, master of the tanker *Prestige*, continue their efforts to have his bail conditions eased while he awaits trial. The master is still required to remain in Spain and report weekly to police, despite having deposited a US$3.6 million bail. His treatment has been widely criticized. This is not least because, under Spanish law, people aged 70 or over have strong grounds to avoid prison sentences if ultimately found guilty. Capt. Mangouras celebrate[s] his 70th birthday next week (Lloyds Agency, 2005l, 1).

The Bahamas Maritime Authority opined in March of 2003 that:

> Another tragedy in this whole saga was the detention of *Prestige*'s master for two months without any justification. BMA's investigation found that the Master risked his life by remaining on board to assist in connecting a salvage tug. The Bahamas made every effort, through diplomatic channels, to have the Master released, yet they met with scant success. He has now (Mar. 2003) been freed on bail set at three million Euros (BMA, 2003, 1).

Yet the Master's detention has wider implications. Now that fewer so-called first-world seamen are devoting their working lives to merchant-marine careers afloat, new, developing-world seamen predominate. Is it fair that Europe or the U.S. detain these sailors indefinitely due to structural failure of their vessel? Could this not lead to some seamen refusing rescue, if what greets them at the end of the helicopter ride is a jail cell? So far Captain Mangouras has not found his place of refuge in Spain – rather, he found himself a squalid cell block, at best a gilded cage, and an expensive one at that. This has raised concern among the maritime community. Renown shipping columnist Grey notes;

> The plight of Captain Apostolos Mangouras, late of the *Prestige* ...firmly moved the issue of the criminalization of the seafarer into the public arena. ...While the draconian powers of U.S. lawmakers is usually cited, the situation in France has come to the fore, with regular incidents in that country's maritime courts, which now have the powers to fine and jail those responsible for pollution, and where huge penalties are being levied. We have seen the growth of the 'blame culture,' in which the whole notion of an 'accident' has become redundant and antipathetic to those who operate in its wake. Provisions such as the *'Erika* Packages' produced by the European Commission, and the demands for accelerated phasing out of single hulled ships after the *Prestige* were little more than slogans that were easily digestible by the public, but had no conceivable relevance to the loss of the *Prestige* itself. It is a cynical and possibly unworthy view that lawyers, politicians and the media, three categories of people who have been greatly active in encouraging this societal change, are perhaps least effected by it!
>
> The way in which loss of life at sea is seen to be of passing interest, while accidental pollution is

regarded as a crime against humanity is surely
indicative of skewed values. Seafarers caught up in
maritime accidents [are] held in legal limbo, and often
become little more than hostages as lengthy legal
proceedings are worked out (Grey, 2005, 18-19).

In another article, the ISU is even more strident in casting
the blame on the Spanish – something it purported not to do while
taking the high road, like IMO, in earlier public reports:

It has been estimated that the cost of a
successful [*Prestige*] salvage, ending in a ship-to-ship
transfer of the cargo at a sheltered location, would
have been no more than €15 million. Localized
pollution might have resulted in costs of up to €35
million. The difference between €50 million and €1
billion or more demonstrates the cost-effectiveness of
salvage. It also underlines the potentially disastrous
consequences of failing to listen to professional
salvage advice. The Spanish are alone in their
insistence that they took the right decision in refusing
shelter for the *Prestige*. In February 2004 a new
Spanish Government Decree was adopted. The
Spanish authorities can now demand the surrender of
legitimate rights of limitation (as provided for under
international conventions). This measure amounts to a
blanket ban on casualties seeking refuge along the
Spanish coastline (ISU, 2005, 5-6).

The first two *Erika* Packages were subsequently modified
after intense lobbying by IMO to disparage and discredit the
European Commission, which had executive authority (Lloyd's
List, 2005c). However, the effects of the *Prestige* further
galvanized authorities in the IMO to action:

Following the loss of the *Prestige*, the countries of the European Union (EU) together with the European Commission, proposed a series of amendments to the 1978 MARPOL Convention. Six EU members also proposed the establishment of Particularly Sensitive Sea Areas (PSSA) covering the Atlantic coast of Europe and the English Channel, with an Associated Protected Measure to ban the carriage of Heavy Grades of Oil in single hull tankers [like *Erika* and *Prestige*] through these areas. The principle of PSSA was accepted, on condition that a ban on single hull tankers carrying certain oils was dropped (IMO Bulletin, 2003, 6).

In a move of almost effrontery, considering that no salvors in this survey are known to have been detained or arrested by Spain, the ISU reacted to Spain's Royal Decree by informing its members that in the event any ISU personnel are detained by a coastal state, all work on that salvage is to stop (except emergency and contractual). This amounts to an effective boycott. Members who work in or for the arresting country face the threat of expulsion from the salvage union (ISU, 2004k); this is saber-rattling. As mentioned in the conclusion, the silence between Spain and the ISU is deafening. Aside from attending the same conferences (i.e.: at the IMO), there seems to be very little direct communication between ISU and Spain, a situation that can only impede cooperation.

CHAPTER 8

ANALYSES OF SUB-HYPOTHESES

Testing of Six Sub-Hypotheses

Re-Statement of Six Sub-Hypotheses

H-1) To protect the environment, an LOF must protect salvors, and SCOPIC does.

H-2) The *Castor* episode exposed fatal flaws in Convention Articles 13 and 14.

H-3) IMO's Places of Refuge are designed to prevent a new *Prestige*, and will do so.

H-4) The *Erika, Castor*, and *Prestige* incidents have influenced new laws and policy.

H-5) Certain countries can be relied upon to offer or deny places of refuge in future.

H-6) The popularity of IMO's Resolution will ensure its success over Spain's Decree.

Testing of Sub-Hypothesis One

H-1) To protect the environment, an LOF must protect salvors, and SCOPIC does.

To test this hypothesis, actual results speak the loudest. In a Herculean effort lasting nearly two months, salvors enabled *Castor*'s cargo to be offloaded while underway, in essentially hostile seaways, and succeeded against immense odds in salvaging the hull and machinery. As a net result, however, Tsavliris were denied their just reward because of the confusion and ambiguity latent in Articles 13 and 14 of the Salvage Convention. The sense of injustice is palpable in the dozens of industry and scholarly articles written during the incident and arbitration. The reaction from all parties seems to be that Tsavliris lost their windfall because they were not covered, by SCOPIC, for their environmental damage mitigation.

Link Tsavliris' failure with *Castor* with Semco's failure to obtain their just desert for the *Nagasaki Spirit* salvage, and the two cases become a highly damning, concrete evidence that Articles 13 and 14 simply do not protect salvors sufficiently to justify the risks and expenses they undertake to save the environment. Without commercial salvors, most coastal states would be at a serious disadvantage in dealing with emergency casualties off their shores, France, with Les Abeilles, being one exception. Without SCOPIC, IMO's Places of Refuge would probably have less force, in the absence of sufficient profit-driven commercial salvors willing to protect the environment since the only tugs available would be those of the host government.

As a direct result of the *Castor* award-reduction, one of the most active salvors in Europe if not the world (Tsavliris), threatened to withdraw from the market altogether (Lloyd's Agency, 2005, 4). Very few coastal states can afford to maintain deep-sea salvage tugs standing at ready off their coasts. Despite thousands of shipwrecks in Galicia over the years, including many major ones, Spain does not yet provide the salvage equivalent of Les Abeilles for their corner of the Bay of Biscay, though the *Ria De Vigo* did an excellent job reaching the Prestige in less than four hours. It would be patently unwise, from an environmental standpoint as well as an economic one, to deprive salvors of financial incentive.

Mergers between salvage companies this century are evidence of consolidation, a tendency of salvors to lease equipment on location, rather than bear the expense of year-round ownership. Salvors now spread their assets through a network of partnerships, rather than geographic clusters. These are all functions of deteriorating market conditions in the industry, brought about by improved safety regulations (CMA, 2005). Deny salvors their percentage, and the world's oceans risk losing them, or creating an expensive salvage hegemony. As seen in the presentation of the history and precedents of salvage law, going back to ancient

Greece and Roman times, it is sensible public policy to reward risk-taking salvors for their efforts and expenses, and has been for centuries. In a modern context, SCOPIC achieves the protection that salvors seek.

Given the immense cost of oil spills to all of those effected, it would seem necessary to keep such a reward system up to date and as trouble-free as possible. Compared with Articles 13 and 14, SCOPIC patently sets out to achieve this. The one-page format, coupled with the statistically insignificant times that published SCOPIC awards have been challenged speaks favorably of SCOPIC. It is clear that working under the Salvage Convention proved very costly to *Castor*'s salvors, SCOPIC has proved satisfactory to the more than one hundred salvors who have worked under it since 1999.

SCOPIC was necessary to replace Articles 13 and 14 and reward salvors, whether the ship is saved or not, for their part in mitigating pollution damage. Without an incentive, salvors may not undertake work of salving derelict hulls, which, because they are unmanned, cannot claim *force majeure*, and are treated like pariahs by coastal states. SCOPIC is incentive-based, results oriented, and based on the 'carrot' rather than the 'stick' approach. The ISU has extensive statistics showing how many tens of thousands of tons of pollutants they have mitigated from the environment. P&I Clubs have been in the fore in SCOPIC and lobbying. In fact, Lloyd's of London, who are also underwriters, attach SCOPIC to their own LOF 2000 form. Lloyd's and P&I clubs were seminal in producing the SCOPIC Clause, which by its very name is geared toward Protection and Indemnity.

There is no doubt, from the statistics and analysis, and a study of the *Castor* case that insurers, and governments of coastal states, have to permit salvors a just reward as an incentive and that salvors provide a statistically significant contribution towards preventing or mitigating environmental damage from seaborne oil pollution.

It is good public policy and common sense to ensure reliable rewards to the salvors who have the expertise and equipment to quickly remove environmentally hazardous cargoes and vessels away from coastal states' waters quickly and efficiently. Failure to do so, whether due to using the Salvage Convention's Article 13 and 14 or otherwise, could deprive coastal states of the most effective anti-pollution facility available to them. This arguments extends to ensuring that the salvage master and crew do not unwittingly become targets of criminal punishment for their work in the line of duty. Punitive measures can have a deterrent and chilling effect on response times to casualties, and the willingness of salvors to travel to certain coastal states. It is simply good environmental policy to reward salvors. Despite their rhetoric, salvors are the partners of coastal states in protecting the environment. A good salvor can negate or diminish the need to divert costly armies of clean-up teams along the coastline every time the wind shifts. *Conclusion:* Hypothesis supported.

Testing of Sub-Hypothesis Two

H-2) The *Castor* episode exposed fatal flaws in Convention Articles 13 and 14.

The *Castor* incident can be seen as a catalyst in favor of SCOPIC. The incidences of utilization of SCOPIC have risen almost one hundred-fold since the *Castor* episode and since SCOPIC 2000 became widely available. For a number of reason, perhaps the most important of which is its simplicity and clarity alongside the timeless Lloyd's Open Form, and because of its effective use in protecting the *Prestige* salvors, SCOPIC has been, if not universally accepted, then widely relied upon in cases where environmental damage may result. The fact that, in contrast to the *Castor* salvors, the *Prestige* salvors have not protested publicly for their remuneration under SCOPIC, added to the general dearth of complaints about SCOPIC by both end-users (clients and salvors) speaks volumes.

This hypothesis can be tested by contrasting the *Castor* and *Prestige* cases. It is important to extract and share with the reader specific conflicts between the now superceded Articles 13 and 14 and the SCOPIC clause - keeping in mind that parties do have the option of which format to contract under. This research helps to explain why Articles 13 and 14 have been superceded by using professional inputs and debate, and also illustrates the argument, and comparison between the contractual texts.

The *Castor* case is a glaring example of leaving not only the abandoned wreck and its owners out in the cold, but salvors as well. The hypothesis is that SCOPIC is an improvement over pre-existing salvage clauses, and will possibly prevent or at least mitigate further major oil pollution incidents, provided the IMO Places of Refuge Resolution achieves anything. The clause-by-clause contrast between the two documents in the Literature Review section serve as an important foundation to the reader's understanding. These building blocks lead to the ultimate question of what to do, once the salvor has been protected, about protecting the environment as well? This is where the IMO Resolution segways, and provides a possible denouement for which the Royal Decree is regrettably a sticking point.

The two documents – Spain's and IMO's - are so inherently at odds with one another that a bridge of some sort; common, mutually agreed maritime law such as *force majeure*, or one of the bundles of laws in the *Erika* Packages, to bridge the two sides into a common camp of ideas and concerns. Apparently their professed shared concern for the environment is not enough to bring the two sides together at this time. Both sides write about the need for dialogue, yet do not seem to act on it. There is a dearth of records showing meetings between Spain, ISU, or BMA officials.

The failure of Articles 13 and 14 are borne out by the facts of Tsavliris' Castor legal case, in which the salvor ultimately lost most of its reward in an arbitration decision. SCOPIC 2000 was in force at the time of the *Castor* case. Salvors and Owner agreed not to be bound by it. That was, in retrospect, the root cause of Tsavliris' loss. As with the *Nagasaki Spirit* case, the owner opted for the Article 13 and 14 award system, from which they ultimately benefited. The sections providing close analysis of these Articles, as well as contrast with SCOPIC, and the section devoted specifically to the *Castor* incident and its legal and financial aftermath cover this question to such a degree that it should be clearly evident to the reader.

The *Castor* incident was so egregious and shocking, to legislators and the general public alike (though it was not as photogenic as the *Erika* and *Prestige* sinking), that it galvanized authorities towards superceding Articles 13 and 14 led to a more ready acceptance of SCOPIC 2000 as a viable alternative, which would protect both salvors and the environment. Furthermore, the *Castor* episode has had a marked effect in developing the IMO's Places of Refuge Resolution, as can be determined from the myriad references to it and the *Prestige* incident, which it preceded by mere months.

Castor was an important incident to illustrate the vulnerabilities of the Articles 13 and 14, and to provide a more secure regulatory safety net for salvors. It surely must be a poor show when one of the most active salvors signs away his profit, based on a contract that he and his colleagues had helped to draft. The *Castor* case is the classic illustration of this. After six weeks of effort, the salvor lost more than a third of the award. The *Nagasaki Spirit* proved also that these Article 13 and 14 awards reduce great salvage work to a maze of accounting exercises (Parry, 1999), which, unlike Lloyd's Open Form is neither simple, clear nor direct.

The *Castor* incident may well have signaled the death knoll of Articles 13 & 14. Data provided by Lloyd's Agency of London indicate that since SCOPIC took effect in 2000, there have been no appeals of those awards published. For the five-year period preceding it (1995-1999), of nine salvages covered by Article 14, six were appealed, or two thirds as many as SCOPIC (Lloyd's Agency, 2005).

All indicia are that, based on the *Castor* salvor's experience, Article 13 and 14 salvage awards were due to be replaced by a more clear, concise and manageable system for rewarding salvors. *Castor* galvanized many, including those who spend more time in parliament than on the bridge, towards reform. Fortunately SCOPIC had already passed (1999) and has been gaining significant momentum. Perhaps some of this shift is attributable to Tsavliris' loss. After significant lobbying, in light of deteriorating market conditions for emergency salvors, SCOPIC seems to have provided the effective cover and assurances that the salvage industry, in particular casualty salvors, as opposed to those engaged in wreck removal and towing contracts, had sought. Not only the spectacular salvage but the stunningly poor reward combined to turn the tide in favor or doing away with LOF's reliance on Articles 13 and 14. *Conclusion:* Hypothesis supported.

Testing of Sub-Hypothesis Three

H-3) IMO's Places of Refuge are designed to prevent a new *Prestige* and will.

Although IMO's Places of Refuge Resolution is fairly recent, there have been sufficient voluntary denials and grants of refuge over the past quarter-century to test this hypothesis. Despite the best intentions and its timely issuance, the IMO Resolution is still just that – a mere resolution. Unlike binding state or international law, the resolution is as much a recommendation as anything else. Coastal states still retain the rights to police and protect their sovereign shores. This is evidenced by Spain's recent enactment of a Royal Decree, or national law, asserting the nation's right to deny any vessel with or without cause, access to their places and ports of refuge.

The fact that Spain has exercised this power several times since last year on *Nestor C*, and MSC *Carla* (whose owners were forced to submit a $1 million Euro bond to approach Galicia for engine repairs), confirm this point. By way of contrast, Spain has rejected seven of eight ships seeking refuge, whereby the U.K. have accepted twelve of the fifteen that sought refuge. While there have been commendable efforts by countries, such as the U.K. and Norway, to designate and publish certain places of refuge available to international shipping, these are not binding.

The coastal state retains the right, fundamentally, to reject or accept vessels to its shores. Such a decision is grounded in internationally accepted and binding law, namely IMO's Intervention Convention, MARPOL 1978, and OPRC 1990 (IMO, 2005a). Ironically, these laws stemmed from coastal states wanting to primarily keep refuge-seeking ships away from their shores during the comparative blitzkrieg of oil spills of the 1970s. IMO's Resolution swings the pendulum back towards more of a balance, but it is not enough to supplant Spain's Royal Decree and its kin at this time.

Some of this hypothesis is obviously hyperbolic. There has not been an exact repeat of the *Prestige* facts since, though the 66 examples do provide some strikingly similar incidents, without the catastrophic loss of oil. The case studies of *Ikan Tanda*, the fertilizer ship forced out of Cape Town by port authorities that drifted to within ten miles of port, and then broke apart in 2001, and *Princess Eva* that was brought to safe anchorage off Ireland in 2004 to perform STS operations are two examples with very differing results.

Despite the thrust of the overall hypothesis (that IMO's Resolution will be a cure-all for ships in distress, and for salvors under SCOPIC), it seems unlikely that the IMO Resolution has the force of legal mandate to prevent another *Prestige* from occurring. In similar circumstances, if the government of Spain wishes to hold to their Royal Decree and demand extortionate and usurious bonds from shipowners on perhaps impossibly short notice in order for Spain to avail itself of their ports, it is likely that a *Prestige* incident could well be replicated. The essence of an effective LOF is simplicity and clarity; of a good SOSREP unfettered implementation of decisions. In comparison, Spain's Decree is obstructive at best to notions of both speed and efficiency.

Spain is the first coastal sate to have really sharpened the incisors of legislation regarding places of refuge. The legal landscape for crew and owners of disabled ships in the region has actually been made much tougher by the Royal Decree. This has happened since the *Prestige*, despite, or perhaps in direct counter-point to, IMO's well-intended Resolution. Whether enough political pressure could be brought to bear on Spain in the event of a repeat of *Prestige*-like incidents, in light of the actual results of their refusal to offer that ship refuge, remains to be seen, and cannot be clearly answered in a paper dealing with known events which have already occurred. The inference, however, is that yes, a repeat of the *Prestige* could well re-occur of the coast of Spain at any time, so long as the one party (Spain) that could prevent such an occurrence by offering refuge, seems unwilling to do so. As a positive development towards achieving uniformity, IMO's Resolution and the *Erika* Packages have encouraged coastal states to develop their own command-and-control-structure; Minister of Marine in Ireland, SOSREP in the U.K., South Africa's Marine Safety Authority (SAMSA), and the Maritime Prefect in France.

Differentiation between numerous layers of laws reveals that while the IMO has the potential to decree binding international standards and laws (i.e. to enforce Plimsoll marks, investigate ship classification, manning, or SOLAS compliance), this particular Resolution does not enjoy the same force of law. This reality is borne out in the case studies, as vessels continue to be turned away by one or more coastal states, even under force of arms. Tellingly, no punishments are meted out to coastal states aside from the ordinary course of political reshuffling.

Despite the best intentions, and a self-proclaimed emphasis on the practical aspects of efficient salvage and pollution mitigation, the fact remains that the IMO Places of Refuge Resolution is little more than a non-binding suggestion – not even a request. Despite the decades of tanker spills, this concept is still in its infancy. It may be another generation and perhaps another spate of *Prestige*-like spills before the Resolution becomes enforceable. Meanwhile the resolution lives up to its legislative intent in word only, and not necessarily in deed. It is essentially, and sadly, a toothless tiger. *Conclusion:* Hypothesis rejected.

Testing of Sub-Hypothesis Four:

H-4) The *Erika, Castor*, and *Prestige* incidents influenced practice and policy.

Erika alone has had three eponymous bundles of laws presented by the European Commission (the three *Erika* Packages) to the European Union Parliament, since 2000, whereas no law has been named for the *Torrey Canyon, Titanic, Exxon Valdez*, or *Estonia*. The sheer volume of data that these three shipwrecks together have generated have an immense and immediate impact on European maritime policy. They have effected what types of ship transit European waters (accelerated double-hull program), what routes they use (Norway has tried to push their territorial sea to 12 miles to keep Russian winter traffic offshore), and what kind of command-and-control structures and information-sharing, particularly across borders, takes place. (France and Germany are examples of progress in this direction).

It is evident that the *Erika* and *Prestige* mishaps were catalysts, especially for France and the European Union to reform shipping industry and standards, which the IMO fought tooth and nail. The effort was successful at least inasmuch as Europe has since agreed on a gradual phase-out of single-hulled tankers transiting their waters. (CMA, 2004). The *Erika* and *Prestige* spills serve as the kind of touchstone that the *Exxon Valdez* did in formulating the Oil Pollution Act (OPA), of 1990, just as the *Titanic* disaster led to the Safety of Life at Sea (SOLAS) Convention and improved Marconi codification, the *Amoco Cadiz* and *Torrey Canyon* disasters in the English Channel prompted the 1969 CLC Convention; International Convention for Civil Liability for Oil Pollution, for preventing shipowners from limiting liability to the value of the ship after salvage based on the Limited Liability Act of 1851 (46 USC 181-189).

Thanks to *Erika*, Europe's single-hull legislation is now more stringent and accelerated than their counterparts in the U.S., where such reforms were checked by the holding in <u>U.S. v. Locke</u>

in 2001. The U.K., Denmark, Germany, Norway, New Zealand and others are moving forward with listing places of refuge (Tradewinds, 2005, 42). In the alternate, French and Spanish discussions regarding *Prestige* led to a virtual diplomatic *impasse* (Lloyd's Agency, 2005b, 12). And in 2004 the EU voted not to disclose lists of places of refuge (Lloyd's List, 2005).

By whatever unfortunate coincidence, these three major oil-tanker mishaps within a specified geographical area, half a dozen countries in Europe and northern Africa found themselves being made the doormat to oil from three tankers in as many years. These consecutive mishaps, though not as grand in scale as the massive ULCCs and VLCCs of the 1960s and 1970s, seem to have had the accumulative impact of a *Torrey Canyon* (119,000 tons) or an *Amoco Cadiz* (223,000 tons). Taken in aggregate, the *Erika*, *Castor*, and *Prestige* casualties totaled a threat of 137,000 tons. Given the huge reduction in oil pollution by volume since the 1970s, when placed contextually this trilogy would qualify as being of equal significance to either of these giants of European oil tanker spills.

The element of temporal spacing may provide another reason – for those three to four years, especially factoring the *Prestige* continuing bled dirty cargo over a period of years from its dormant hull. Europe, particularly the Bay of Biscay, was faced with the prospect of oil pollution essentially year-round for several years. No wonder the Biarritz beachgoers develop oil-spill-related '*psychoses*' (Tayler, 2004). *Conclusion:* Hypothesis supported.

Testing of Sub-Hypothesis Five

H-5) Certain countries can be relied upon to offer, or deny, refuge in future.

This hypothesis is not borne out by data showing 66 actual instances of granting or denial of places of refuge. The behavior of coastal states is sporadic at best. Only the U.K. seems to be consistently welcoming (15 grants versus only three denials), whereas Spain seems to be the most hostile to potentially dangerous ships in their waters. Seven out of eight Spanish responses having been to send the ship away. Each nation has exhibited clearly contradictory behavior. After going to the assistance of a disabled LPG tanker *Henrietta Kosan* off its Galician coast, Spain subsequently required a Euro $1 million bond of a ship carrying containers (MSC *Carla*) with mere engine trouble. While the U.K. has recently helped a number of vessels to find and utilize places of refuge, it has also denied such vessels as *Aeolian Sky*, which was a general cargo ship sunk of the U.K. coast for lack of a place of refuge.

Of 42 countries in the 66-case survey, a full eleven of those 'doubled' their roles, leaving only 31 in the survey. By eliminating one-case countries such as Namibia, Cape Verde, Benin, Togo, Ghana, Nigeria, Malaysia, Bermuda, Dominican Republic, Netherlands Antilles, Malta, Gibraltar, Tunisia, Yugoslavia, Sweden, Cyprus, and New Zealand, (a further 17 countries), there are only 14 countries left.

Of these, a core group of eleven countries have unpredictable patterns, and they are along the busiest shipping routes: U.K., Ireland, Belgium, France, Spain, South Africa, Portugal, Australia, Indonesia, Haiti, and the U.S.. Certain countries could be categorized as unlikely to offer refuge based on their existing records – Morocco, Brazil, Senegal and Sri Lanka, and Singapore, with two denials each and no offers to grant refuge. Spain would be included, based on its 80 percent or so rejection record. However, this would be erroneous since Spain (LPG ship *Henrietta Kosan*), like Portugal, with four rejections and one noteworthy welcome (*Nestor C*) has shown a propensity for unanticipated reversals.

In sum, out of the eleven countries left in the survey, most only rarely handle places of refuge issues, and have not built up enough of a record to extrapolate with any reliability what their behavior is likely to be. This included Belgium, Haiti, and Indonesia, which have only denied or granted one refuge each, effectively neutralizing themselves into a placebo class. Though it would be pat to say that the U.K. is likely to offer refuge and that Spain is not likely to, these presumptions are so easily and readily disproved that it would be prejudicial at best and untenable in general to do so. The variables are very fluid, and Spain could match U.K.'s record or visa versa, in weeks.

Interestingly, the data reveals that a small group of eight states actually handled 59, or 90 percent, of the 66 casualties, which suggests that for reasons of politics, geography, or chance, some countries are much more active with refuge than others, and, *ergo*, that refuge might be better sought in some places than in other. This is, of course somewhat conjectural. The seven countries in question are the U.K., Spain, Portugal, France, the U.S., South Africa, and Ireland, with three or more each. It must be admitted that a large portion of the case studies, roughly two thirds of the raw data were the result of an official questionnaire sent by the Comite Maritime International. The criteria for answering were quite subjective; participants could fill in the blanks with refuges that country had offered, or others it had denied, or they could, as many did, simply not answer. The questionnaire can be self-aggrandizing or, alternately, somewhat incriminating (in the eyes of their peers if nothing else). The counterpoint to this, however is the fact that new inputs can be plugged in at any time, based on past, present or future incidents, depending on criteria. The barge cases were admittedly a stretch, as they sought to actually discharge their cargo on land, accounting for about ten countries between them.

The easier way to access a coastal state's propensity to either accept or reject vessels in distress would be for them to post this information and make it known, particularly to commercial and recreational ships. Since your average voyager will not seek out CMI's three-year-old study, transmitting such information via the internet, Navtex, daily VHF or SSB broadcasts, or nautical email updates, as are sent by the USCG regarding closures and openings of various channels and canals, might be a solution.

Better yet, a so-called neutral party, such as the IMO, Greenpeace, or another organization, could receive, maintain and promulgate this information. In 2004, however, European parliament specifically voted against a law requiring or requesting coastal states to release such information (Lloyd's List, 2005). So far, countries that have listed places of refuge are, in order of first to last: Indonesia; a paid STS site off Singapore and Malacca in February 2003; Denmark, tentatively in August of 2003, but they then redacted it; Germany was on the cusp of passing a five-state Baltic plan including places of refuge designations in March 2004; Spain deigned itself ready to release its list in April 2004; the U.K. in February 2005; Norway on January 2005; and New Zealand, somewhat inadvertently on the heels of the *Capella Voyager* grounding in Whangarei in April 2003. *Cappella*'s grounding was really a case of *force majeure*; the ship was entering the harbor bar when holed; turning to exit would have meant more damage.

Despite all this helpful information on a half-dozen brave countries, none of them are obliged in any way to permit vessels refuge on their coasts. So even though some lists might be public, they are not necessarily binding. The intent as regards the IMO Resolution, is to build momentum, consensus, and some uniformity over time so that the issue receives its steady share of coverage. So there is hope for more contributions in the future. Doubtless each state has its own pre-determined list already for response plans as part of Naval or Coast Guard defense. The host country, of course, is likely to know the coastline of their own country better than most visiting salvors.

Given available data, there seems no reliable way to predict coastal states' places of refuge behavior based on past performance. This is most likely tied in to Hypothesis three, in which it is surmised that coastal states are still legally able to hold their own counsel as regards granting or denying refuge. Since states have no legal obligation to uniformly welcome troubled ships, except in cases of *force majeure*, for example, in which case there is often no timely opportunity to deny access, states also do not have an obligation to advertise or promote themselves as prone to react in a certain way. Besides which, doing so could invite trouble in the form of disabled tankers. Though the location of breakdowns are happenstance, heavier-trafficked areas adjacent to land are vulnerable.

This conclusion ties into the overall hypothesis, that whether regulated or not, coastal states are most likely to react on a case-by-case basis according to their assessment of the risk and comfort level with a number of inputs, including environmental damage and political consequences. The criteria are too subjective to base a reliable prediction upon, and the law is too weak and contradictory. Ironically, IMO alone holds the field both for promoting and quashing Places of Refuge, by virtue of having promulgated the Intervention Convention in the 1970s.
Conclusion: Hypothesis rejected.

Testing of Sub-Hypothesis Six

H-6) The popularity of IMO's Resolution will ensure it trumps Spain's Decree.

Despite the galvanizing effect that the trio of oil incidents (*Erika, Castor*, and *Prestige*) seems to have had, and the general hue and cry against Spain for its unwelcoming stance and Royal Decree, the IMO Resolution is in reality not likely to change much except people's awareness of the problem, and coordination of damage control between otherwise disparate control- centers. In the case of Spain versus the ISU and IMO, the Resolution seems to have obstructed, rather than cleared channels of communication. This was presumably not the drafter's intent. Ironically, like the *Castor* it spurned, Spain has become a pariah-state in the maritime community, only able to muster up three disparate nations – Mexico, Argentina, and Dominica, to its support during its latest effort to influence the EC (Lloyd's List, 2004).

As discussed in hypothesis five (countries can be relied upon to grant or deny refuge in a rational, predictable manner), the evidence in 66 case studies suggests that despite the best planning, coastal states tend to make their final decision either during a crisis or after one has developed. For many coastal states, the choices are bleak: they are essentially painted into a corner before they start.

The *Prestige* incident in particular is on the way to overtaking *Erika* and *Castor* in that it focuses regional (EU) and world attention on the dilemma of abandoned tankers in environmentally and economically rich coastal areas. These incidents have led directly to IMO Resolutions (MAS included) to deal with such incidents in the future, forcing a thorough re-appraisal of existing laws as they relate to such casualties. The newest tests of IMO and Spanish laws are few and generally very recent.

Both *Castor* and *Prestige* have played a major role in galvanizing legislative attention and avoiding repeats of these mishaps. This is borne out by the profusion of literature on these cases in many legislative and executive exchanges, as well as the continuing cleanup and litigation costs involved in the *Prestige* aftermath itself.

The *Prestige* incident itself and the major political and economic backlash and penalties which it brought in its wake has had an indelible effect on the Spanish government's psyche, and on how they chose to react in the future, including formulation of the Royal Decree. This seems still to steer them on their own course towards an all-out ban of sub-standard ships along their coast. (Spain is not alone; Bermuda insists on a roughly 24-mile curtilage enforced on all ships transiting the island, based on the number of vessels which have strayed onto its reefs while using the island as a waypoint). Ironically, Spain's Royal Decree, charging bond for all ships requesting refuge, may turn out to be the most lasting legacy of the *Prestige* spill and IMO's Resolution.

Despite the apparent support for IMO's Places of Refuge Resolution, the fundamental question of whether to welcome or spurn a leaking tanker ultimately has less to do with popularity than with pollution control and politics. Spills as harmful as that caused by *Prestige* or *Erika* can even drive a wedge between neighbors, as between France and Spain. Analysis of the way a sampling of some 41 countries reacted to past tanker casualty cases are not reliable indices of how they may act in the future. So long as the IMO Resolution is little more than a toothless tiger, the Spanish Royal Decree has the weight of the law behind it. For now, that is the balance achieved, and it favors Spain, not the 164 other IMO signatories. *Conclusion:* Hypothesis rejected.

Summary

Re-Statement of Six Sub-Hypotheses

H-1) To protect the environment, an LOF must protect salvors, and SCOPIC does.
Conclusion: Supported. The *Castor* outcome, versus the *Prestige* award, affirms this. If salvors cannot be assured of a reward for their risk, particularly when a third party (coastal state) effectively condemns the ship, removing that element of profit from the salvor's control, it becomes necessary for shore-bound lawmakers to ensure the water-borne salvor loses only the ship, and not the special compensation reward with it. Otherwise al participants risk losing salvors or facing a small hegemonic cabal of them.

H-2) The *Castor* episode exposed fatal flaws in Convention Articles 13 and 14.
Conclusion: Supported. Compared with the Article 13 and 14 awards and appealed awards of the *Castor* and *Nagasaki Spirit* salves, SCOPIC produces the results salvors sought: reward money for helping to save the environment.

H-3) IMO's Places of Refuge are designed to prevent a new *Prestige*, and will do so.
Conclusion: Rejected. Despite the best intentions, IMO's Places of Refuge Resolution simply lacks the force to supervene of law of other laws binding on nations (i.e. Spain), unions (i.e. the European Union), and international bodies (i.e. the IMO's own Intervention Convention from a previous era). This body of maritime law is not ripe enough yet to be bent in favor of so small

a segment as salvors, as against the national governments of 185 nations. Against the world lobby, an association of several hundred salvors (ISU) can only do so much, even if they have a media advantage. Though the ISU's advertising is as enrapturing to the public, legislatures, and environmentalists alike as an *Erika* or *Prestige* catastrophe, it is not enough to create policy beyond, say, SCOPIC revisions. A country like Spain has more assets to protect than a salvage company, and IMO and Spain have more constituents than ISU.

H-4) The *Erika, Castor*, and *Prestige* accidents influenced practice and policy.
Conclusion: Supported. The effects of this trilogy of oil spills have had a very real and tangible impact not only on most of the shorelines of Europe, having kept the continent under assault for nearly three continuous years. These spills have captured and focused reform efforts in such a sustained manner that it could be several decades until there are any series of mishaps like it. These casualties are really a big three, up there with Bhopal, Chernobyl, and the Zeppelin *Hindenburg*, in that they galvanize a long-sweltering regulatory impulse and channeled it towards a series of three noteworthy new laws: the *Erika* Packages, Places of Refuge Resolution, and Spain's Royal Decree. The question remaining is whether these laws will prevent or actually require another series of similar calamities in order to achieve the same legislative focus in the future.

H-5) Certain countries can be relied upon to offer or deny refuge in the future.
Conclusion: Rejected. The data are insufficient to enable such an extrapolation. The behavior of national governments, in some cases through nominated maritime administrators, is too erratic, at times irrational and contradictory, to provide any reliable sense of direction. This remains true even for the select few nations who have very active records in the field of refuge issuance and denial, namely the U.K. and Spain (together handling 22 out of 66 of the

cases (roughly 30 percent), though they are only two nations out of 42 (about two percent) of the countries surveyed.

Even a survey going back 30 years, based on raw data ostensibly from each individual country (CMI, 2002), provides an insufficient indicator of which direction any one country is likely to go when faced with its next casualty. This conclusion reinforces the notion that, for now at least, so long as hypotheses three and six are rejected, (i.e. presuming that one cannot prevent another *Prestige*, and Spain's Decree trumps IMO's Resolution). It is unreasonable to expect countries to react in ways that may be deemed morally appropriate, when there is no legal penalty for that coastal state to act otherwise. In essence, Spain's concept of the stick (punishment) method of disincentive seems, according to the methodology, to be more effective than IMO's carrot (reward), incentive and inducement-driven strategy.

Put another way, governments, like the ships they seek to regulate, are run by humans, with inherent inconsistencies and errors in judgment. Both participants – ship and state – are subject to the same irrationalities and inconsistencies. The law as it stands allows individual countries like Spain to march to their own drum. No law, short of one banning ships altogether, will ever outlaw shipwrecks, which in today's context implies oil spills as well, since most vessels carry oils of some sort. As long as ships propel themselves with oil and carry oil or oil-derivative cargoes, there will be oil spills.
Spain and any other sovereign nation can respond to this reality as they choose.

H-6) The popularity of IMO's Resolution ensures it will trump Spain's Decree
Conclusion: Rejected. No amount of popularity overcomes the legal superiority of Spain's Royal Decree. One has the force of law, the other – IMO's Resolution – has the force of a well-thought-out and polite request. Any nation that chooses to 'ignore their mother's well-meant advice' is free to do so.

As the *Prestige* spill demonstrates, however, the Winter

North Atlantic (Plimsoll's most dangerous rankings of sea conditions, which overwhelmed both *Erika* and *Prestige*) is not a consequence-free environment where governments can order tanker ships and salvors around. Spain and her citizens will be paying the price for their poor judgment on the *Prestige* three years ago for several years yet. They are likely, as indicated by their suing the ABS for US$5 billion, try to bring as many others with them as possible. Under SCOPIC the salvors, at least, should be in the clear. This time.

Rejection of Three of Six Hypotheses

Despite a clear predilection to present a paper damning to the authorities in Spain and in defense of salvors (the author is from the flag-state of the *Prestige,* the Bahamas, and for three years ran a fleet of tankers, creating an inherent bias), the evidence gathered from extensive and specific case studies, as well as industry and media coverage, when applied through the methodology model outlined in this paper, leads to the conclusion that half of the hypotheses are rejected. In some ways the methodology is similar to that used by the IMO with Places of Refuge: come up with a good idea, float the idea to interested parties, gather as much data and as many media inputs as possible, debate the idea, and then come to conclusions on which to base a writing. The arguments in favor of SCOPIC (which gained supremacy over Article 14 awards while the paper was being written) and against the Salvage Convention, were expected to be fairly well defendable and, perhaps by chance, aided by the *Castor* case, proved to be. The other three hypotheses failed to a surprising degree.

The depth to which the trilogy of mishaps have embedded itself on the European psyche and legal library is still somewhat overwhelming. It is evident from media coverage that *Erika* and

Prestige in particular have left a lasting and painful impression in a significant portion of the European population, judging from how much has been written about it. At least a portion of this fascination with these wrecks is the amazing conditions which permitted an airborne photographer to capture the final moments of both vessels, turning their death-throes into quite a public event, capturing the public's morbid fascination like the photographs catching HIV patients taking their last breath in the 1980s.

The ISU has reacted stringently to Spain's $500-million-dollar penalty scheme, which seems inescapably to have been tailored as a direct challenge to Places of Refuge:

> The Spanish Government's decision to put a half-billion-dollar price-tag on a place of refuge for ships in distress is counter-productive and in some situations could actually increase the threat to the environment. Commenting on a new Spanish Decree requiring a €415.2 million financial guarantee for entry into a place of refuge, ISU President Joop Timmermans said: "The Spanish appear to have learnt nothing from the devastating *Prestige* spill. If anything, this 'Spanish Solution' actually makes a repeat of the *Prestige* disaster more likely.
>
> After the *Prestige* experience, it should be obvious that there are situations where the only way to save a laden tanker with severe damage is to grant immediate access to a place of refuge. It is hard to imagine how a demand for the surrender of rights, under international conventions, to limit liability will contribute to prompt decisions on requests for shelter. Indeed, this approach is likely to increase the number of lepers of the sea. This unhelpful Spanish Decree could also stand in the way of the salvor attempting to use his best endeavors, as required under the Salvage

173

Convention 1989 and LOF, to prevent pollution; a
salvor is unlikely to be able to meet [such a high]
demand (Timmermans, 2004, 6).

The fact that the IMO Resolution, so well touted during,
and immediately following, its recent debut, would in reality lose
its promise when quickly challenged by Spain's Royal Decree
must have been a disappointment to its drafters. The rationale and
logic behind the Places of Refuge Resolution, especially as
illustrated in cases, seem to hold wide appeal except for certain
coastal states. Perhaps if these states were rewarded, like salvors,
their attitudes to ships in distress would change. But then again, the
prospect of slamming the front door on an, undesirable, if not
outright dangerous visitor (read: vessel) may have an equal, if less
socially acceptable, appeal.

The sub-theme of the whole second half of the paper, once
the discussion moves beyond SCOPIC and salvors, is where the
IMO Resolution will take us. In truth, it does not take us very far.
It's more of a scenic route; its balms are more prophylactic than
surgical. The conclusion of the paper hinges on interpreting the
data and past experience as well as the legislative record, to
anticipate how the IMO resolution will hold up.

The more effective approach at this time may be to
recognize the effectiveness of the stick incentive, but opt for a
carrot approach, trying to bring Spain closer to the bargaining
table. A combination of political pressure and environmental
outrage has encouraged a number of countries to be proactive and
develop their own places of refuge and strategies for dealing for
environmental calamities. What remains to be seen is which will
gain the most following soonest; laying out, or pulling up, the
welcoming mat. The coastal states, not the shipowners, ship
regulators, and Masters, seem to have the shoe on their foot for
now.

The evidence garnered indicates that Spain and other
coastal states are free to do as they wish as regards places of
refuge. They can shoo away potentially dangerous ships using a

massive bond as a Damoclean sword, as with MSC *Carla*, or hang out the mistletoe and extend a conditional welcome, as Spain recently did, when they sent a tug to assist the *Henrietta Hosan*, a potentially dangerous gas tanker. The data suggest that since 40 ships were welcomed and only 26 were denied refuge, there is almost double chance of being provided a place of refuge as there is of being denied. This speaks favorably to human nature and to the notion that, as a matter of customary practice, most ships will be given the benefit of the doubt when in distress. It is also noteworthy that Spain accused Captains transiting their shores of lying about the condition of their vessels. This suggests further that there needs to be some bridge-building with the nation most set against places of refuge. Certainly Masters and the shipowners and operators who advise them should be candid with their host nations, and not obfuscate in the midst of a crisis. A call for better communication by IMO or ISU applies to all parties equally.

By their harsh reaction to Spain's legal maneuvers, the ISU, IMO and P&I clubs, as well as the EC and EU risk alienating, through blame, one of the important players. There seems to exist a real need for both sides – ISU/IMO and Spain, to reacquaint themselves with each other and open a dialogue at a less dizzying height than the President Chirac of France to Prime Minister Aznar communiqués which apparently took place during Prestige, resulting in a course change by tugs to the west, sealing the tanker's fate. Failure of either side to initiate dialogue until the next calamity would be a very regrettable missed opportunity. The risk of fines may rise as a result, and many participants and lobbyists may be the losers. Taken in larger context, if some spills like *Prestige* do end up costing several billion U.S. or Euro dollars, is it really so unreasonable that Spain require up to a $500 million deposit against possible future mitigation? Bonds for crew and vessels in ports are certainly not new, especially in the post-9/11 security environment.

Since at least the 1990s, various conventions (CLC, TOVALOP, ITOPF) have required tankers to carry up to $700 million pollution liability. In the U.S., there is even a superfund, which accrues with every ship call in the country. Though a huge disincentive, is Spain's Decree much more than a cost-prohibitive door fee? The notion that shipowners who cannot afford Spain will limp on to the nearest neighbor is a thorny one, not least because this will often simply be impossible. Then what? That is beyond the purview of this paper, but if Spain has learned anything from the *Prestige* calamity, the government will think twice before sending a disabled ship offshore, in the hopes that, as with *Castor*, it will sail over the horizon, enter other backyards, and bother other countries.

Another aspect is that, based on the case studies analyzed, Spain, France, and Portugal tend to vote to ban vessels more often *en bloc* than not. What one votes, the others generally back up. Thus, a tanker disabled off Finisterre has a very long way to go to find a friendly coast. The data suggests that Morocco would not be ideal to find refuge, the Canaries, Madeira and Azores islands are all controlled by the same triumvirate. Though it may mean re-crossing the Bay of Biscay (which probably caused the mishap), the U.K. might be the safest bet for refuge. As discussed, however, the data are woefully inconclusive on this point.

Seen in a circumspect way, Spain, despite being treated like a pariah by the media, ISU and IMO, may not be that far off track after all. Certainly it appears that, for all its faults, the Spanish Decree has the force of law. Its tiger is fully teethed. That recognition alone should tighten up ship-performance around Spain, could increase salvage coverage of the area, and may lead to improvements in La Coruna's physical port; $500 million is earmarked to expand the outer harbor. However, there is no doubt that no legislation or law will prevent oil spills in the future, whether from double-hulled state-of-the-art tankers or single-hulled bulkers, which along with breakbulk, roro, woodchip, reefers and myriad other vessels carry 90 percent of the worlds' commerce.

It is noteworthy that within two years of the *Prestige* mishap, but 30 years following the much-published *Urquiola* spill of 101,000 tons there in 1976, Spain has blown up five pinnacles of rock at the harbor entrance of La Coruna to facilitate access to the dangerous channel on which so many other ships, including the *Aegean Sea* (80,000 tons), in 1992, have come to grief (Fairplay, 2003, 25). Doubtless, political pressures both within Galicia and outside of Spain's borders (the EC, France, and IMO), have had a combined effect on that nation's policy. Nevertheless, the inescapable fact seems to be that the IMO resolution remains essentially unenforceable, and each country, whether in the European Union or not, retains the sovereignty to determine who crosses their aquatic, as well as terrestrial, borders. No mere resolution has - or perhaps will - change that.

CHAPTER 9

CONCLUSION

Overall, SCOPIC can be seen as a working arrangement satisfactory to owners and salvors who share the common goal of mitigating pollution damage, and associated expenses, once a potentially dire ship-in-distress situation exists. Inasmuch it continues to reward salvors, as LOF has for over a century, SCOPIC works. Though admittedly all its kinks as regards application of compensation have yet to be ironed out, an agreed-upon arbitration panel has been resolving most cases amicably (Short, 2003, 1).

In the salvage industry, as mentioned, there has been a marked shift from savings lives and ships to protecting coasts. This is an evolving necessity, and one which ISU is now promoting, as one of the few ways the industry has to remain viable is through SCOPIC compensation. The traditional 'wait and pounce' salvage strategies that had professional oceangoing tugs stationed at chokepoints in days of yore have given way to government subsidized tugs (like those owned by Les Abeilles in France) and significant amalgamation within the industry.

Three of the six hypotheses deal with protecting salvors to protect the environment. In conclusion, it seems that salvors are truly covered by SCOPIC, and that they can continue at their work reasonably confident in fair remuneration for the risks they take. As far as the other hypotheses effecting salvors, in truth, it seems that it does not really matter, from a strictly 'payment due' perspective, whether a coastal state grants or denies a place of refuge. Either way, the salvor keeps on working until the object of the salve is either corrected and reinserted into the stream of commerce, or, like the *Erika* and *Prestige*, sinks. Either way, SCOPIC is there as an increasingly-utilized option to cover the parties to the LOF.

Shipowners, insurers, and governments will need to continue to offer incentives to salvors. Otherwise they risk being left high and dry, holding the bill for the enormous cleanup costs associated with major pollution incidents. The *Exxon Valdez* spill is estimated to have cost Exxon over US$3 billion; most companies (even governments) could not survive such a payout. In 2004 alone, ISU members salved more than three times the oil spilled by *Exxon Valdez* (1989), *Sea Empress* (1996), and *Braer* (1993) (Figure 2). Added to the US$1 billion, which salvors saved customers in 2001, salvors are evidently a good friend of the environment. Governments and insurers can retain the invaluable services of salvors through cooperation and continued incentives (ISU, 2005).

Of course, put in perspective with the $5 billion that the *Prestige* disaster may cost, and the $5 billion that Spain is asking for (but is not likely to get) from the ABS, these hitherto-record-setting figures pale in comparison. At the outset of this research in 2003, it seemed that the WWF and others were saber-rattling and scare-mongering when they bandied around the $5 billion figure for *Prestige* remediation and settlement. The reality is that those figures are no longer a joke. The way the ship was lost, and that the cargo kept coming back to the Spanish coast seemed uncannily bad fortune (or was it instant Karma following Spain's rejection of the *Castor* the year before?). And what of Spain's neighbors, who pay for Spain's misjudgments? The pat pollution funds and governments who assured neighbors that all would be paid for seem to have run low on funds rather quickly. Perhaps it is time for Europe's superfund?

SCOPIC provides salvors with some of the sense of security, which they sought from Article 14 ambiguities. The alternatives are an inadequate salvage fleet - not entirely unforeseeable, given a further change for the worse in salvors' cost/benefit analyses. Public outcry against environmental pollution has become such a real political force as to require continued, healthy existence of salvage fleets. A major player on the shipowning side sees much of the shipping industry's problems as ones of perception. Though president of one of the world's largest fleets, he also sees it as at least partially self-inflicted. This criticism of shipowners as political entities (Intertanko being foremost, but IMO, flag states, and to a lesser extent P&I Clubs, all as shipowner's lobbyists) comes from an unlikely source. His name is Helmut Sohmen. He is the nineteen-year president of Worldwide Shipping of Hong Kong, and Chairman of the Independent Tanker Owners Association (Intertanko).

Writes Gimbel; "Mr. Sohmen is busily considering ways the [shipping] industry can shed its reputation as a sitting target for environmentalists. He thinks shipowners have not done enough to shake a dirty image:"

> There is nothing in the public mind that would generate feelings of goodwill or warmth towards a metal box that is three months out at sea, but there is a pretty strong response when you get the tar balls and the dead sea birds on your favorite beach. [Sohmen] thinks the shipping industry lacks leadership and political engagement, not least because, over the years, shipowners have maximized their freedom from tax liabilities. This has made the industry something of an outcast. If you don't contribute to national coffers, you don't have much political clout (Gimbel, 2004, 7).

Irrespective of improvements to vessels and training, it is the nature of the maritime environment that accidents will continue to occur. The ISU, underwriters, P&I Clubs, and some governments recognize this. Together, they have been effectively anticipating the need not only for salvors, but also of their own indispensable role in mitigation of environmental pollution.

Spain's Royal Decree brings the Places of Refuge debate into the present. It has not yet been thoroughly tested, and may not be, to the extent of another *Prestige, Castor*, or *Erika*, for years.

The battle lines, between IMO's consensus for Places of Refuge and Spain's insistence on going its own way, have been drawn. Doubtlessly there will be allies on either side. Already Mexico, Dominican Republic, and several other of Iberia's former dependents have fallen into line in support of Spain. On the leading edge of providing (though only very hesitantly publishing) lists of possible Places of Refuge are Norway, Ireland, the U.K., Singapore, Denmark, and a host of other nations. So far, one hundred and eleven states have already signed the Resolution.

Speaking from the salvors corner, the ISU President has this parting volley:

> The *Prestige* spill disaster will cost over €1 billion, perhaps as much as €5 billion. The *Prestige* could have been saved, but only following a tow to a place of refuge. The cost of salvage and pollution damage (on a much smaller scale) would have been in the region of €50 million at most. Having gambled by turning the *Prestige* away – and losing up to €5 billion in the process – the Spanish have now made their position worse. In practical terms, a demand for a huge financial guarantee amounts to a blanket ban on shelter along the Spanish coast. This could contribute to a re-run of the *Prestige* – in Spanish waters, or in the waters of neighboring Coastal States. It places neighboring Coastal States at risk.

> We must hope that other EU member-states will recognize the folly of this heavy-handed approach. It is self-defeating and could well lead to the ultimate absurdity: a Salvage Master having to watch a laden tanker sink, a few miles off the coast, while the parties involved argue about money. Nothing could be further from the spirit of Lloyd's Form (ISU, 2005j, 7).

Overall, the parties covered in this analysis seem cognizant of the risks and rewards at stake, particularly those coastal states that have had to respond to massive oil spills on their coasts. The shipowning and salvage side, while adopting to stringent new regulations, seem to be effectively stabilizing their industry, while at the same time adapting to the new environmental focus required of them now and in the future. Their continuing to do so will be a benefit to citizens, visitors, and users of the marine environment, both ashore and afloat. As evidenced in the *Prestige* case, failure to cooperate with salvors could result in enduring pollution crises, with widening environmental, and thus political, fallout. The salvage industry is finally catching up. Now it is up to the governments of coastal states to pitch in.

BIBLIOGRAPHY

- American Club P&I Club (1999), Circular 99/99, July 12, 1999, "Amendment to LOF Salvage Agreement," http://www.american-club.com/circulars/cir9-99.htm
- BMA, Bahamas Maritime Authority, (2003), The Flag, The Newsletter of the Bahamas Maritime Authority, March, Issue No. 12, p.1
- Bartholomew, John C., (1974), The World Atlas, Bartholomew & Son Edinburgh, U.K..
- Besco, (2005) German photo website, www.besco.de/images/used_marine/vessels/tanker/ erika (Figure 1: Photographs of MT *Erika* Sinking, 1999)
- Bishop, Archie; (2000) "Salvage: Revised LOF 2000 Proves an Asset," Lloyd's List International, London, Sept. 1. Lloyd's of London Press Ltd., London.
- Bourbon Maritime, France (2005), "Offshore Towage and Salvage: Les Abeilles International," www.bourbon-maritime.com
- "The *Blackwall*," (1869) 77 U.S. 1 (Mem), 19 L.Ed. 870, 10 Wall 1 (December term)
- Brice, Geoffrey, Q.C. (1999) "The Law of Salvage: A Time for Change? No Cure-No Pay No Good?," 73 Tulane Law Review, p.1831, May/June
- British Maritime Law Association (BMLA), (2004) "Places of Refuge," MJ Lacey, Meeting 30 March 2004, www.iml.soton.ac.uk/professional_courses/Lacey.doc +bmla+mjl&hl=en
- Browne, Ben (2001) "Places of Refuge – The IUMI Solution," IUMI (International Union of Marine Insurance) Meeting, Genoa Italy 16-19 Sept.. www.iumi.com
- Buckley, Michael (2001), "The Origins of Lloyd's Form," Published in ISU Bulletin 20, Oct. 2001, pp.1-5, www.marine-salvagae.com/media_m03.htm

- CEDRE (2005), French environmental organization, www.le-cedre.fr, Paris, France
- Churchill, Professor Robin & Lowe, A. V. (1999), The Law of the Sea, Third Ed., Juris Publishing, Manchester Univ. Press, p.356.
- Comerma, Eric, PhD. (2005), Universidad Politechnica de Cataluna in Spain, eric_comerma@yahoo.es, c/o Felicia, URI Ma.MA candidate, Kingston, RI.
- CMA, Connecticut Maritime Association, CMA Shipping (2005, 2004, 2003); Author attended each year and gleaned much useful information from delegates and attendees.
- CMI, *Comite Maritime International*, (2002) "Places of Refuge: Report of the CMI to the IMO Part II," 83rd Session of the IMO Legal Committee, Paris, France, September.
- CNN.com, (2005), Photograph repository, www.icnn.net/cnn.net/cnninteractive (Fig. 7)
- Corrosion Doctors, (2005) website, Figure 1, www.corrosion-doctors.org, *Prestige*
- Deutsche Well, (2005), German web news agency, www.dw-world.de/dw/image (Fig. 7)
- Donaldson, Lord, of Lymington, (1999) "The Donaldson Report: Command and Control: Report of Lord Donaldson's Review of Salvage and Intervention and their Command and Control, 1999" [26 recommendations following the *Sea Empress* oil spill in Milford Haven in Feb. 1996]. dft.gov.uk/stellent/groups/dft_shipping/documents/page
- Donaldson, Lord, of Lymington, (1994), "Donaldson Inquiry, MT *Braer*," May 1994 for the U.K. Government - see MAIB Report, and UK Department of Transport web site, www.dft.gov.uk, www.wildlife.shetland.co.uk
- Dunn, Russell B. (1996), Direct U.S. Maritime Subsidies: Recurrent Influential Factors and Trends, Master's Thesis and Proposal, Marine Affairs Department, U.R.I., Kingston

- Edwards, Bernard (1994), S.O.S.: Men Against the Sea, New Guild Books, Dorset, U.K.
- In Re *Exxon Valdez*, (2001) AMD 1, 270 F.3d 1215.
- Fairplay (2001a), The International Shipping Weekly, Redhill, Surrey, UK, "*Tanda* reveals African experience – SAMSA demands iron-clad guarantees," 22 Nov., p. 41.
- Fairplay (2003b), The International Shipping Weekly, Redhill, Surrey, U.K., "Rock extracted from a hard place," 19 June, p. 25.
- Fairplay (2004c), The International Shipping Weekly, Redhill, Surrey, U.K.
- "Desperately seeking *Erika*: The *Erika II* Package," 5 Feb., Vol. 350, pp. 16-19
- Farrington, Karen, (1999), Shipwrecks, Thunder Bay Press, London, U.K.
- Felsted, Andrea (1999a), "Donaldson Report Prompts Further Scrutiny of SCOPIC," Mar. 18, 1999, Lloyd's List International, London, Lloyd's of London Press Ltd., UK
- Felsted, Andrea (1999b), "SCOPIC is Invoked for the First Time," Apr. 17, Lloyd's List International, Lloyd's of London Press Ltd., London, U.K..
- Felsted, Andrea (1999c), "SCOPIC Code of Practice to Benefit All, Says International Group," June 28, Lloyd's List International, Lloyd's of London Press Ltd., London, U.K..
- Flayhard, William, (2003), Perils of the Atlantic: Steamship Disasters, 1850 to Present, W. W. Norton, New York and London
- Gibbs, Jim (1971), Disaster Log of Ships, Bonanza Books, Crown Publishers, New York
- Gaston, Jack; (2000), "Booming Tsavliris Set to Beat Salvage Record," Oct. 20. Lloyd's List International, Lloyd's of London Press Ltd., London, UK.

- Gimbel, Florian, (2004) "A Perfect Mix of Oil and Water: The World's Biggest Private Shipowner is in the Vanguard of an Industry Overhauling Itself," Financial Times, London, 25 Oct., p. 7.
- Gilmore, Grant, and Black, Charles L. Jr. (1957), The Law of Admiralty, 7th Edition, 1971, The Foundation Press, Brooklyn, NY, US.
- Goodacre, S.B., (1999), "Not Quite A Good Week for Salvors," Letter to the Editor, Mar. 26, Lloyd's List International, Lloyd's of London Press Ltd., London, UK.
- Gould, Circuit Judge, (2003), Bartholomew v. Crowley Marine Services, Inc. 2003, D.C. No. CV-00-091670-WTM, No. 02-35364, United States Court of Appeals for the Ninth Circuit, Seattle WA, June 5.
- Greenpeace, (2003), "Return to Sender; Chronology," www.essentialaction.org/ return.chron.html, New York, NY.
- Grey, Michael (2005), "The Criminalization of the Seafarer," BIMCO Bulletin, Vol. 100, No.1, p.18
- Grotius, Hugo, (1633) The Freedom of the Seas, or *Mare Liberum*, Garoffin, Ralph Van Deman, Ed., 1916 Edition, Oxford University Press, New York, NY.
- Guillen, A.V., (2004) "Prestige and the Law: Regulations and Compensation," Proceedings of the 17th Annual Conference on Oil Pollution, 2004, Claims Handling and Cleanup Response, London, 15-16 Mar., Lloyd's List Events, London, U.K..
- Haine, Edgar A., (1983), Disaster at Sea, Cornwall Books, East Brunswick, NJ, U.S.
- Hamon, Herve, (2003) "The Abeille d'Quessant," Maritime Life and Traditions, No.18, Spring, p.11, and www.bourbon-maritime.com/ang/metiers/sauv.html.
- Harvey, Richard (1999) "SCOPIC Clause Just Needs the Finishing Touch," Oct 27, Lloyd's List International, London, Lloyd's of London Press Ltd., London, UK.

- Hayward, Steven, (1999), "NIMBYism and the Garbage Barge From Hell," Editorial, www.ashbrook.org.
- Hix, Nikki D. (2002), <u>West</u> <u>Coast</u> <u>Port</u> <u>Development:</u> <u>Mitigating</u> <u>Impacts</u> <u>from</u> <u>Dredging</u>, Thesis, Marine Affairs Department, U.R.I, Kingston RI.
- Hughes, David (2003), "Salvors Want to be Paid More for Protecting the Environment," <u>The</u> <u>Business</u> <u>Times</u> <u>Singapore</u>, Singapore Press Holdings Ltd., Apr. 7.
- ISL, Institute of Shipping Economics and Logistics (2005), Bremen, Germany, isl.org/products_services/publications/samples/COMMEN T-3_2004.shtml
- INTERTANKO, International Association of Independent Tanker Owners, (2005), www.intertanko.org, "Source of Oil Pollution Into the Sea," (Tanker Accidents 3%)
- International Maritime Organization, IMO, (2005a) London, England, www.imo.org,
- "Places of Refuge - Addressing the Problem of Providing Places of Refuge to Vessels in Distress," and related links, www.imo.org/Safety/mainframe.asp , U.K..
- International Maritime Organization, (2005b), London, England, www.imo.org, "*Prestige* Aftermath - IMO Confirms Readiness for Swift Response," IMO News, No. 1, p. 6.
- International Maritime Organization, IMO, (2005c), London, UK, www.imo.org/safety
- "Resolution A.949(23); Guidelines on Places of Refuge for Ships in Need of Assistance," ('Places of Refuge Resolution'), 5 Dec., p. 1.
- International Maritime Organization, IMO, (2005d), London, UK, www.imo.org/safety
- "Resolution A.950(23); Maritime Assistance Service," (MAS) 5 Dec., p.1
- International Maritime Organization, IMO, (2005e), London, UK, www.imo.org

- "French Group Raises *Prestige/Erika* Issues with IMO," IMO News No. 1, p. 29.
- International Maritime Organization, IMO, (2005f), London, UK, www.imo.org/safety
- "Background on Places of Refuge," pp.1-3.
- International Maritime Organization, IMO, (2004g) London, UK, www.imo.org/safety
- "Places of Refuge," IMO News, No.1, p. 18.
- International Oil Pollution Compensation Fund (OIPC) (2005), www.iopcfund.org.
- International Salvage Convention (1989), "London Salvage Convention", Adopted 28 April 1989, Entered into Force 14 Jul. 1996, www.imo.org/conventions.
- International Salvage Union (ISU), (2005a), official web site: www.marine-salvage.com
- "ISU Annual Statistical Survey," since 1978.
- International Salvage Union (ISU), (2005b), official web site: www.marine-salvage.com
- "Casualty Salvage."
- International Salvage Union (ISU), (2005c), official web site: www.marine-salvage.com
- "Appendix - Annual Pollution Prevention Survey," (2001, 2002, 2003)
- International Salvage Union (ISU), (2005d), official web site: www.marine-salvage.com,
- "Overview."
- International Salvage Union (ISU), (2005e), official web site: www.marine-salvage.com,
- "Media Information: ISU Meeting, Quebec," Sept. 16, 2002
- International Salvage Union (ISU), (2005f), official web site: www.marine-salvage.com,
- "ISU Facts."

- International Salvage Union (ISU), (2004g), www.marine-salvage.com/media_f03.htm,
- "ISU Pollution Survey Highlights Decline in Salvage," Mar. 16, pp.1-3.
- International Salvage Union (ISU), (2004h), www.marine-salvage.com/media_n03.htm
- "ISU Salvors Launch New Drive to Prevent Marine Pollution," Sept. 22, pp.1-4.
- International Salvage Union (ISU), (2001i), www.marine-salvage.com/media_m03.htm
- Buckley, Michael, "The Origins of Lloyd's Form," ISU Bulletin 20, Oct., pp.1-5.
- International Salvage Union (ISU), (2001j), www.marine-salvage.com/media_d03.htm
- "Salvors Warn: Spain's Place of Refuge Decree is 'Self-Defeating,' Mar. 1, pp.1-2
- International Salvage Union (ISU), (2004k), www.marine_salvage.com/media_e03.htm, Timmermans, Joop, "Salvage Remuneration: Building on the Past, Finding New Solutions," Lloyd's Maritime Academy, International P&I Conference, Sep. 13-14, pp1-9
- International Salvage Union (ISU), (2004l), www.marine_salvage.com/mediac03.htm, Timmermans, Joop, "Safe Havens: Some Important Lessons from the *Prestige* Affair," International Harbor Master's Association Congress, Bremen, May 23-28, pp. 1-8.
- Internattional Salvage Union (ISU), (2004m), www.marine_salvage.com/pollution.htm "Pollution Defense; Preventing Marine Spills," pp. 1-6.
- IUMI (International Union of Marine Insurance) (2001), Meeting, Genoa Italy 16-19 Sept., www.iumi.com
- Independent Tanker Owners Oil Pollution Fund (ITOPF) (2005), www.itopf.com/ stats.html, "Historical Data: Case Histories," Apr. 8.

- Kemp, Peter (Ed.) (1988), The Oxford Companion to Ships and the Sea, Oxford University Press, (1st Ed. 1976, paperback), Oxford, U.K.
- Kendall, Lane C., and Buckley, James J., (2001) <u>The Business of Shipping</u>, Cornell Maritime Press, Centreville, MD, US. (First Edition 1972).
- Lacey, Michael J. (2004), "Places of Refuge," British Maritime Law Association (BMLA), Meeting 30 March 2004, www.iml.soton.ac.uk/professional.courses/Lacey.doc
- +bmla+mjl&hl=en
- Langewiesche, William, (2004), <u>The Outlaw Sea: A World of Freedom, Chaos, and Crime</u>, North Point Press, Farrar, Straus, and Giroux, New York, NY, US.
- Lloyd's Agency Salvage Arbitration Branch, (2005a), www.lloydsagency.com/ Agency/Salvage.nsf, 2005, London (LOF records of casualties going back to 1980's)
- *Castor*: full report of casualty and arbitration, 2002 onwards, www.lloydsagency.com /agency/salvage.nsf/lusearch/ - "Salvage Arbitration", keyword 'castor', 'Case Report'
- (Reports "with kind permission of Lloyd's Casualty Desk") last report Aug. 27 2004
- Lloyd's Agency Salvage Arbitration Branch, (2005b), www.lloydsagency.com London
- *Prestige*: full report of casualty and arbitration, 2002 onwards, www.lloydsagency.com/agency/salvage.nsf/lusearch/ - "Salvage Arbitration", keyword 'Prestige', under 'Case Report' - last report as at March 2005 was dated Nov. 5, 2004
- Lloyd's Agency Salvage Arbitration Branch, (2005c), www.lloydsagency.com London
- "LOF Facts and Figures," London, UK, www.lloydsagency.com to April 2005

- Lloyd's Agency Salvage Arbitration Branch, (2005d), www.lloydsagency.com London
- "Lloyd's Open Form" tab, 2005
- Lloyd's Agency Salvage Arbitration Branch, (2005e), www.lloydsagency.com London
- "LOF At Work," London, UK, www.lloydsagency.com to April 2005
- Lloyd's List International, (1999a), Lloyd's of London Press Ltd., London, "Owners Must Keep an Eye on SCOPIC Clause: Insurers and Salvors not in Agreement," Mar. 9.
- Lloyd's List International, (2000b), Lloyd's of London Press Ltd., London, "BV [Bureau Veritas], says refuge port could have saved lost *Treasure*," 26 June, p. 5.
- Lloyd's List International, (2000c), Lloyd's of London Press Ltd., London, "Sea Change for Salvage Industry," Dec. 16.
- Lloyd's List International, (2001d), Lloyd's of London Press Ltd., London, "A problem of definition with damaged ships and ports of refuge," 16 Jan., p. 3.
- Lloyd's List International, (2001e), Lloyd's of London Press Ltd., London, "SCOPIC Clause Is No Replacement for Article 14," Mar. 14.
- Lloyd's List International, (2001f), Lloyd's of London Press Ltd., London, "Nigeria to take in refugees ship," [*Alnar*], 21 June, p. 5
- Lloyd's List International, (2001g), Lloyd's of London Press Ltd., London, "Ex-*Regent Sea* sinks on way to breakers," [The *Sea*] 16 July, p. 1.
- Lloyd's List International, (2002h), Lloyd's of London Press Ltd., London, "*Castor* Case Raises Question of Degree of Risk," Aug, 27
- Lloyd's List International, (2003i), Lloyd's of London Press Ltd., London, "Editorial: The Irish show the way," [*Princess Eva*], 10 February, p. 7.

- Lloyd's List International, (2003j), Lloyd's of London Press Ltd., London, "Letter: *Erika* was not refused place of refuge," 12 February, p. 5.
- Lloyd's List International, (2003k), Lloyd's of London Press Ltd., London, "Norway names ship refuge agency," 23 April, p. 3.
- Lloyd's List International, (2003l), Lloyd's of London Press Ltd., London, "Digest Makes Arbitration Verdicts Clear," Apr. 28, p. 16.
- Lloyd's List International, (2003m), Lloyd's of London Press Ltd., London, "Editorial: Hospitality: Hong Kong's willingness to accept the *Bunga Melawis Satu*" 6 May, p. 7.
- Lloyd's List International, (2003n), Lloyd's of London Press Ltd., London, "Operator identifies five possible havens for doomed tanker," 1 July, p 3.
- Lloyd's List International, (2003o), Lloyd's of London Press Ltd., London, "Unease as Danish authorities seek to sell refuge proposals," 4 August, p 1.
- Lloyd's List International, (2003p), Lloyd's of London Press Ltd., London, "Salvors seek to foster closer ties with the wider shipping industry," Nov. 28.
- Lloyd's List International, (2004q), Lloyd's of London Press Ltd., London, "Association Adjusts to Pondering a Protocol for Casualties," Mar. 11.
- Lloyd's List International, (2004r), Lloyd's of London Press Ltd., London, "Germany in port of refuge move," 18 March, p. 3.
- Lloyd's List International, (2003s), Lloyd's of London Press Ltd., London, "Spain under fire for 'nimby' approach; Spain's new Decree on Places of Refuge," 19 April, p. 11.
- Lloyd's List International, (2003t), Lloyd's of London Press Ltd., London, "Spain's secret list of 35 places of refuge raises eyebrows," 19 Apr. p 14.

- Lloyd's List International, (2003u), Lloyd's of London Press Ltd., London, "No strings as Spanish tug aids LPG carrier," [*Henrietta Hosan*], 21 April, p 3.
- Lloyd's List International, (2003v), Lloyd's of London Press Ltd., London, "MSC pays E1m bond in first for Spanish rules on places of refuge," [MSC *Carla*], 14 June, p, 1.
- Lloyd's List International, (2003w), Lloyd's of London Press Ltd., London, "P&I clubs offer financial guarantee for places of refuge," 25 Oct., p 6.
- Lloyd's List International, (2003x), Lloyd's of London Press Ltd., London, "Honolulu berth reserved for adrift *Hanjin Pretoria* as tug nears boxship," 21 Dec., p.1.
- Lloyd's List International, (2005y), Lloyd's of London Press Ltd., London, "Initiatives That Could Change the Future of Shipping," Mar. 15, Erika Photo
- Lloyd's List International, (2004z), Lloyd's of London Press Ltd., London, "Spanish Ship's Refuge Decree Has Cash Sting," 18 Feb. p.3
- Lloyd's List International, (2003aa), Lloyd's of London Press Ltd., London, "Pleas from the Spanish Suffer Refuge Defeat," 2 Jun., p 1.
- Lloyd's List International, (2003bb), Lloyd's of London Press Ltd., London, "Initiative that Could Change the Future of Shipping," 15 Mar., p 1.
- Lloyd's Open Form (LOF 2000) (2005), www.lloydsagency.com, 2005
- Lloyd's Ship Manager (2000)'"*Treasure*" sinking forces refuge debate'. Sept., p 5.
- Lowry, Nigel, with Brian Reyes and Sandra Speares, (2002), "Shock as *Castor*'s Salvor has Award Slashed by a Third," Lloyd's List International, London, May 23. Lloyd's of London Press Ltd., London, UK.

Tanker Disasters / Eric T. Wiberg

- MAIB - Marine Accident Investigation Branch (UK) (1994), "Report Into the Engine Failure and Subsequent Grounding of the Motor Tanker *Braer* Garth Ness Shetland, 5 Jan. 1993," Southampton UK Dec. 1993 - see also Donaldson (1993).
- Mandaraka-Sheppard, Aleka, (2002), Modern Admiralty Law, With Risk Management Aspects, University College, London, Cavendish Publishing Limited, London-Sydney.
- MARISEC (Maritime International Secretariat Services, Ltd., London, England), (2005), for the International Chamber of Shipping (ISC) and International Shipping Federation (ISF), Shipping and the Environment, Shipping Facts, www.marisec.org/shippingfacts
- Maritime Law Association of the United States (MLA), (2000), "Formal Report of the Committee on Salvage-SCOPIC - Shipowner's Casualty Representative," Doc. No. 750, www.mlaus.org, May 2005.
- Marti, B. (1991), "U.S./Pacific Basin Containerized Trade: Flag of Convenience Participation," 15 Marine Policy, pp.193-198.
- Marti, B. (2004), "Inbound Waterborne Transport of Oil Products to New England," Studies in New England Geography, Number 18, pp.1-27.
- Motor Ship, (2001), '*Treasure* spill raises safe haven issue,' August, pp. 18-19
- Mowat, Farley, (1958), The Grey Seas Under: The Perilous Rescue Mission of a North Atlantic Salvage Tug, First Lyons Press, New York, U.S..
- Mowat, Farley (2001), The Serpent's Coil, Lyon's Press, New York, U.S., (1st Ed. 1961)
- Murray, Christopher F., (2005), "Any Port in a Storm? The Right of Entry of Reasons of *Force Majeure* or Distress in the Wake of the *Erika* and the *Castor*," www.moritzlaw.osu.edu/lawjournal/murray.htm.

194

- Naval Academy Press, (1994), Reassessment of the Marine Salvage Posture of the United States 1994, pp.102-104, Appendix F, www.nap.edu/openbook
- News of the Odd, (2004), "Today in Odd History: Garbage Begins Lengthy Trek (March 22, 1987," www.newsoftheodd.com/article1018.html
- OCIMF, Oil Companies International Marine Forum, (1981), "Disabled Tankers: Report of Studies on Ship Drift and Towage," Witherbys Publishing, London, U.K..
- Oil Spill Intelligence Report, (2002), "Crippled VLCC denied shelter; disaster averted," 16 May, p. 4.
- OPA 1990 (1990), "Oil Pollution Act of 1990," www.us.gov
- Osler, David, (2003), "*Prestige* – 'Cause Unknown,'" Lloyd's List International, London, Apr. 2. Lloyd's of London Press Ltd., London.
- Parry, Phil, (1999), "SCOPIC Becomes a Case of Suck it and See: Compensation," May 19, London, Lloyd's of London Press Ltd., London, Lloyd's List International
- Patterson, Chris (2002), General Manager of Contract Services, Crowley Marine, Seattle WA email to author, Tues. Nov. 25.
- Pearsall, Ronald, (1996), Lost at Sea: Great Shipwrecks of History, Smithmark Publishers, New York, U.S.
- Penelope, Mathew, (2002), "Australian refugee protection in the wake of the *Tampa*" – American Journal of International Law, July, pp. 661-676.
- Prebble, Quentin, (2001), "Ports of Refuge," IUMI (International Union of Marine Insurance) Meeting, Genoa Italy 16-19 Sept., www.iumi.com
- Quinn, William P., (1979), Shipwrecks Around New England, Lower Capt Publishing Co, Orleans MA, U.S.
- Ritchie, David, (1999) Shipwrecks: An Encyclopedia of the World's Worst Disasters at Sea, Checkmark books, New York, NY U.S. (1st Ed. 1996, Paperback)

- Rose, Francis D., Steel, David & Shaw, Richard A.A., Ed.s, (2002), Kennedy and Rose: The Law of Salvage, 6th Ed., "British Shipping Laws", Sweet & Maxwell, London.
- RMS Republic, (2000), "Salvage Law and the Salvors' Compensation," www.rms-republic.com/sal00.html.
- Safe/Sea Online, (2005), www.safesea.com/boating_info/salvage/anderson/awards
- "SCOPIC; Special Compensation P&I [Protection and Indemnity Club] Clause (1999), incorporated a Article 14 of the 1989 Salvage Convention," www.lloydsagency.com, "LOF At Work," "SCOPIC, Forms."
- Safety at Sea, (2001), "The *Tampa* - safe haven or political hunting ground?" Dec., p. 8.
- Seatrends, (2003) "Refuge issue is raised again," [*Capella Voyager*], 2 May, pp 1-2.
- Semco, (2005), "Company Profile," www.semco.com.sg/Salvage_Profile.htm, 8 Apr.
- Semco Salvage and Marine Pte. Ltd. v. Lancer Navigation Co. Ltd. (1997) ["*Nagasaki Spirit*"], House of Lords, 1997 A.C. 455, (Lords MacKay, Goff, Lloyd, Hope).
- Shanley, Capt. Brian G., (1999) The Quest: A Condensed Guide to Shipwrecks and History of Narragansett Bay, Published by its Author, paperback, Jamestown R.I.
- Shipping Facts, (2005), "Shipping and the Environment," Diagram/Pie Chart, www.marisec.org/shippingfacts/enrirmntcontrib.htm
- Short, Ian, (2003) Lloyd's of London Salvage Arbitrator, email to author, Tues. 2 Dec.
- Smit Americas, Inc., for itself and on behalf of Edward J. Hosking, its employee, Plaintiff, v. The MT *Mantinia*, her engines, tackle, machinery and other appurtenances, in Rem., (2003) 259 F. Supp. 2d 118, 2003 AMC 1096.
- Speares, Sandra (1999), "SCOPIC Loopholes Raise Questions Over Usage," Sept. 8. Lloyd's List International, Lloyd's of London Press Ltd., London, U.K..

- Stuart, Denzil (2001), "Underwriters Give LOF and SCOPIC Clause Thumbs-Up," Mar. 19, <u>Lloyd's</u> <u>List</u> <u>International</u>, Lloyd's of London Press Ltd., London, U.K..
- Tayler, Jeffrey, (2004), "In the Wake of the Prestige: Despite Freshly Scoured Beaches, the Politics of Oil Shipping Still Trouble European Waters," Conde Nast Traveller, pp. 80-85, Mar.
- Tetley, William, Prof., (2004), "Glossary of Maritime Law Terms," 2nd Edition, <u>www.mcgill.ca/maritimelaw/glossaries</u> (also emails to author explaining terms).
- Timmermans, Joop (2004a), <u>www.marine_salvage.com/media_e03.htm</u>, "Salvage Remuneration: Building on the Past, Finding New Solutions," Lloyd's Maritime Academy, International P&I Conference, Sep. 13-14, pp.1-9
- Timmermans, Joop (2004b), <u>www.marine_salvage.com/mediac03.htm</u>, "Safe Havens: Some Important Lessons from the Prestige Affair," International Harbour Master's Association Congress, Bremen, May 23-28, pp.1-8
- Tradewinds, (2003a), shipping newspaper, Oslo Norway, <u>www.tradwinds.no</u>, "Galicia planning a port of refuge," 14 March, p. 39.
- Tradewinds, (2003b), shipping newspaper, Oslo Norway, www.tradwinds.no, "Portugal open arms to stricken bulker," [*Nestor C*], 3 January, p. 34.
- <u>Tradewinds</u>, (2005c), shipping newspaper, Oslo Norway, www.tradwinds.no, "Norway Releases Open List for Ports of Refuge," 28 Jan., Vol. 16. No. 4, p.42 Oslo, Norway.
- Tyler, David, (2005) "Retrieving Fuel Oil from the Oceans Depths Required Testing New Salvage Technology," pp.55-56, <u>Professional</u> <u>Mariner</u> #87, Portland ME, Apr/May.

- United States Coast Guard, (2002), "Marine Safety Manual; *Force Majeure*," Vol. VI, Chap. 1, Comite Maritime International, 2002, Annex 4, p.30
- United States v. Locke, Gov. of WA, Et Al. / International Association of Independent Tanker Owners [Intertanko] v. Locke, 529 U.S. 89 (2000).
- Von Glahn, Gerhard, (1996), Law Among Nations: An Introduction to Public and International Law, (1st Ed., 1965), Simon and Schuster, Needham Heights, MA, US.
- Wald, Matthew L., (2004), "Candidates Preach Oil Independence to Unconverted Public," The New York Times, p.A18, Oct. 25.
- White, Stephen F., and Gutoff, Jonathan M., (2004), "Amicus Brief Submitted by C-PORT to the Supreme Court of the United States," www.c-port.org/news/2004-news/Northern-Voyager-SCOTUS.html
- Witte, Arnold, (1998), "Salvors Near Completion of Simplified Contract," Apr. 15. Lloyd's List International, London, Lloyd's of London Press Ltd., London, U.K..
- Woodyard, Doug, (1998), "Special Report on Towage & Salvage: Income Down in Real Terms Despite Record Recoveries," Oct. 29, Lloyd's List International, Lloyd's of London Press Ltd., London, UK.
- WWF (World Wildlife Federation), (2005), panda.org/news_facts/crisis/spain_oil_spill

ACKNOWLEDGMENTS

I would like to thank my parents, Anders and Jane Wiberg of Nassau, Bahamas, first and foremost for supporting me in every way possible during this four-year bid for a better education. For his help and guidance since even before I enrolled at the University of Rhode Island, Professor Bruce Marti deserves my sincere thanks. His patience, inspiration, editing and support over the years as an advisor, fellow mariner, and mentor salvaged my degree. My wife, Alexandra, has been wonderfully understanding and supportive during difficult years while I pursued two degrees, ran two small companies, and wrestled with bar exams.

In the University of Rhode Island's Marine Affairs Department I am grateful to all of the Professors who have taught me, particularly Dr. Pollnac and Professor Marti. For helping to guide me through the URI program, special thanks to Professor Burroughs, Susan Myette, Associate Dean Lynn Pasquerella and Kristine Connery. For salvaging the Marine Affairs Joint-Degree Program, my colleague Terry Boardman, Professor Jonathan Gutoff, and Dean David Logan of Roger Williams University School of Law, deserve special credit. Author Bjorn Turmann inspired me to take the next step in publishing.

In 2002, while I was applying to URI, the *Prestige* was struggling for its life in the North Atlantic, a fact that I mentioned in my student essay. This research, which dovetails with the roughly four tanker casualties I have been involved in, began back then. The best news to come of most of the many casualties mentioned herein is that so few mariners lost their lives.

Eric Wiberg
Kingston RI
May, 2005

199